Putting

the

Pieces

Back Together

ALSO BY MEL LAWRENZ

Patterns: Ways to Develop a God-Filled Life

Mel Lawrenz

Putting
the
Pieces
Back Together

How Real Life and
Real Faith Connect

GRAND RAPIDS, MICHIGAN 49530 USA

ZONDERVAN™

Putting the Pieces Back Together
Copyright © 2005 by Mel Lawrenz

Requests for information should be addressed to:
Zondervan, *Grand Rapids, Michigan 49530*

Library of Congress Cataloging-in-Publication Data

Lawrenz, Mel.
    Putting the pieces back together : how real life and real faith connect /
Mel Lawrenz.
       p. cm.
    ISBN-10: 0-310-25477-9 (hardcover)
    ISBN-13: 978-0-310-25477-5
    1. Christian life. I. Title.
    BV4501.3.L396 2005
    248.8'6—dc22
                                 2004020893

This edition printed on acid-free paper.

Published in association with the literary agency of Alive Communications, Inc., 7680 Goddard Street, Suite 200, Colorado Springs, CO 80920.

Interior design by Beth Shagene

Printed in the United States of America

---

05 06 07 08 09 10 11 12 /❖ DCI/ 10 9 8 7 6 5 4 3 2 1

For Eva
May your life keep coming together
by God's gracious hand

CONTENTS

Part 2

God Puts the Pieces Back Together

Part 3
Living Whole Again

PREFACE

As I wrote this book, I had in mind the people I know who want to get their lives together, which is, of course, pretty much everybody I know.

Together is a crucial word. It expresses our irrepressible hope that we can connect all the roles we have, all the impulses that drive us, all the responsibilities we bear, and all the convictions we commit to. It is also the hope that somehow we can be put back together after the shattering and alienating experiences in life.

Faith and life should connect. They do connect. Our beliefs about God and his ways in the world, about human nature, about the afterlife, and about everything else must cohere if they are true. And they are the building blocks with which we can build a faith we can live in.

So this book is a journey through the major themes of Christian belief as they intersect with real-life issues. The prayer and questions at the end of each chapter are meant to encourage you to take a little open space, a bit of thinking time, to carry these themes to where you live, or to discuss them in a group.

This journey is for you. Whether you feel that your life is a pile of puzzle pieces and you just don't know where to begin, or that you have a basically sound picture of who you are and who God sees you to be, we all need to progress in putting the pieces of our lives together. We will discover realities we never would have imagined and a design for life that God had in mind before we were born.

Part 1

Our Pieces

PIECES OF LIFE

All the king's horses and all the king's men
couldn't put Humpty together again.
— *Nursery rhyme*

L ife would be easier, wouldn't it, if all of its
pieces held together. If they always made
sense. If nothing ever broke off. If no part were
ever lost or twisted or detached.

Imagine life if you could glide smoothly
through the day from one of your roles to the
next: mother to wife to co-manager to next-door
neighbor to aunt to friend; or brother to supervisor to dad to son to church leader. Is there one
person in there somewhere? Is it possible to live
as the same person at home as at work, instead
of civil Jekyll in public and monster Hyde when
you're alone?

Imagine life if no one ever left, if illness never
caused loved ones to drop from our lives, if the
people we care about never died or deserted us.

Imagine life in Paradise. Eden was the wonderful opening chord of life, a complete harmony. Nothing in excess, nothing missing,
nothing broken. But when that break did happen (and what an awful shattering sound it
made), when human beings said, "We think we
can do this on our own," all of creation shud-
dered and cracks spread throughout. Our only

hope from then on was that someone, somewhere, would help us put the pieces back together.

But even when things aren't broken, life often seems to be a pile of pieces we stand looking at, wondering how they all fit together, or if they do. Does what I believe about God have anything to do with how I behave as a citizen? How does my understanding of humanity's purpose fit with my everyday experiences with people in all their glory and shame? How can God be loving and accepting and angry at the same time? How can horrible things happen to people who seem to be no more than innocent bystanders? How does this speck of dust that we call Earth fit in the vast universe? Where is this world heading? What does God want me to do with my life? Does a person's belief about life after death change the atmosphere in the chapel before a funeral starts?

DEATH'S SHATTERING BLOW

I was just four years old when my father suddenly died. What I remember is being at my grandfather and grandmother's house in the country and not returning back home to Chicago for a very long time. How could a four-year-old have handled the scene my mother had to witness? Wheezing and feverish, my father had struggled under the heavy hand of a terrible cold. Feeling a bit better, he decided to walk down to the corner drugstore to pick up some family snapshots that had been processed. Back home, he felt much worse and asked my mother to get him a cup of warm tea. Minutes later she returned to find him slumped in the large, green easy chair, pneumonia having put fluid where air should have passed. And that was that. Twenty-eight years and then, exit.

I don't remember crying then. One of the reasons is that when my father dropped out of my life like a meteor's quick flash in a silent winter sky, the light from other people around me kept burning. Amazingly, they helped put the pieces back together, right away. I was blessed (and certainly don't take it for granted) with a loving mother, and an uncle and two grandparents on my mother's side with whom I already had a strong bond. And the next six years, during which we lived as a three-generation household, was a time when my bones grew, my attitudes formed, and my view of life developed fairly unclouded, but only because loving adults held together my life, which had experienced dismemberment.

Seven or eight years after that, however, I began to see that God the Creator, whom I had believed in but had not really sensed as the powerfully present Father, was really the one putting the pieces back together.

GOD IS ALIVE AND ACTIVE

What a startling awakening it is to find that God is alive and active and that he moves powerfully, sometimes as imperceptibly as the stars but as quickly as a cougar when he wants to.

It's amazing to feel that someone has taken scales off your eyes and, like the blind man Jesus healed, you can see people standing where there were none before (though they may look like trees while your eyes are getting used to the light). And then you discover other people whose eyes have been similarly opened. You find this bond between yourself and others—fathers all about, and mothers and brothers and sisters—all still spiritually gangly and flawed, as human beings always will be, but coming together nonetheless. You find brokenness that you had never noticed before, because the light is helping you see pieces you didn't even know were there. It may sting a bit to see that there are more pieces than you thought, but the Father's presence assures you it's okay. It really will be okay.

ALL THINGS HOLD TOGETHER IN CHRIST

When the Bible says that "in him [that is, Christ], all things hold together," it is describing the fundamental structure of all reality. "All things" means *all* things. Go down to the level of the molecule, then the individual atom, and science will tell you it is a mystery how atoms and their particles hold together. But they do. How is it that when you put into your mouth meat and potatoes and vegetables, they break apart but you yourself don't break apart? Your body keeps reorganizing itself, growing, healing. The biological pieces keep coming together, with some interruptions for illness, until that last breath moves out across your lips and the spirit departs. Only then does your body return to dust.

The divine Christ puts the pieces back together because he put it all together the first time. "He is the image of the invisible God, the firstborn over all creation. For by him all things were created: things in heaven and on earth, visible and invisible, whether thrones or powers or rulers or authorities; all things were created by him and for him. He is before all things, and in him *all things hold together*" (Col. 1:15–17, italics mine).

Our only hope of surviving in a broken, disconnected, fractured world is that God created everything according to a grand pattern. The very meaning of the word *creation* is taking pieces and making a whole. Heaven and earth do fit together, even though it often seems as if they are two different universes. God created the visible and the invisible as one reality, though we so often choose to live merely as bodies without souls. Why, at creation, did it all hold together? Why are there patterns to the pieces? It is because "all things were created *by* him and *for* him" (italics mine).

Tracing Life's Pieces Back to God and His Purposes

When we relate the pieces of life back to God as source and believe that the pieces are there for him and his purposes, we can see the sense in it all.

Regarding the human race, broken into so many pieces, that same passage goes on to say, "[Christ] is the head of the body, the church; he is the beginning and the firstborn from among the dead, so that in everything he might have the supremacy. For God was pleased to have all his fullness dwell in him, and through him *to reconcile to himself* all things, whether things on earth or things in heaven, by making peace through his blood, shed on the cross" (Col. 1:18–20, italics mine).

When one head coordinates and directs a small human community, all the pieces of a new society and a new family—real human beings—should come together. And they do come together because Christ's reconciliation, peace, and blood are real. At the moment of Jesus' crucifixion, when it seemed as if the whole world were falling apart, when he who is good and right was resolutely rejected, humiliated, and then murdered, the reconstruction began. The earth shook and rocks split, and in the temple, the curtain was torn in two from top to bottom, signifying that the division between God and humanity was coming down, that a new way was opening for earth to rejoin heaven.

Are you looking to start foundational construction or make repairs in your life? Those are the two basic ideas in this book: putting pieces together and putting pieces back together. One person in a courtship attempts to fit the pieces together to make a marriage; another attempts to fix a broken marriage. Fit and fix. Pieces put together and pieces put back together. Someone in the first week of a job tries to navigate new territory; someone else has been twenty years on the job and that same week attempts to repair a problem to avoid getting fired. A new believer reads the gospel of John for the first time, fitting Jesus' statements there with other passages about Jesus; a longtime believer shuffles through well-worn pages, scanning for a passage that may build up a discouraged friend. A college freshman is confronted for the first time in philosophy class with the problem of evil; a policeman stands at the scene of a sniper shooting, shaking his head in dismay.

BUILDING THE HOUSE OF FAITH

Our whole lives, we are in the process of building the house of our personal faith and understanding, a house we can seek shelter in when some random hurricane hits. Life would be great if all of it were constructive, if we never had to fix anything. But that's not the way it is; we must build and we must repair. If a person hasn't built something in the first place, it is hard to find shelter when the storms hit.

Years ago I spoke at a shelter for homeless people. A large man in drooping and dark clothes, once a university professor but now a street dweller, sat and played beautifully at the piano. A young man in a dirty yellow jacket sat in a chair against the wall, staring straight ahead. I stepped up to an oak lectern as old men and young men shuffled along the tiled floor to take their seats. I have never been homeless, so I cannot imagine what it must be like to be naked in the world that way. What words would I share with them? This was no day for spiritual clichés or pious platitudes. These men had nothing. The food in their stomachs was a bonus for the day. Some may have wanted to hear words of spiritual truth; others likely did not.

Putting the pieces of personal faith together and building that faith is like finding a home to live in after you have been homeless. You gain a roof over your head to protect you from the elements. Walls set boundaries for the various parts of living. There are places where food and clothes, pots and pans, furniture and linens are organized and stored.

God wants each of us to have a belief system that is not merely a collection of bits and pieces of opinion and conviction. Faith is a great pattern in which specific beliefs fit together in a God-defined design. Like a house constructed from foundation blocks, beams, bricks, and roofing tiles, a personal Christian belief system should have structural integrity, beauty, and practicality.

And how glad we can be that we do not need to make this design. We discover it. Truth is not something we invent. Its attractiveness flows directly from the exquisite personality of God. Its consistency comes from the unchanging character of God. And its practicality comes from the gracious desire of God to give us a home we can live in.

So if you believe in God, the Father Almighty, who made heaven and earth; if you believe in Jesus Christ, God's Son who came to earth; if you believe in the Holy Spirit; and if you believe that we are designed to live as a communion of saints, that forgiveness is the fresh beginning offered by a merciful God, and that there is an everlasting life beyond this Act One of our existence—then you have the foundations of a home you can live in.

And the best thing you can do is to say to God, "Where, dear Lord, do you want to continue the construction of my faith today?"

PRAY THIS

Lord, help me to sort the pieces of my life. I want to have a faith that is certain because it holds together and consistent because it is part of the tapestry of your truth. I want to be a consistent person in all the different roles I have to play in life. I know I need your help with the tremors that have shaken me in the past and that will do so again in the future.

FOR REFLECTION OR DISCUSSION

1. What are some of the pieces of your life that you need to find ways to hold together at this time?
2. How have you experienced your life and faith coming apart?
3. What are some of the ways we experience brokenness that we can do nothing about? What are some of the ways we bring brokenness on ourselves?

WHAT'S WRONG
WITH ME?

I am not a perfect man.
— *U.S. Congressman caught in a moral scandal*

Whenever I hear a public figure defend himself with the oft-repeated words, "I know I'm not a perfect person," I wince. It seems the height of hubris. I feel like saying, "No, the thought never crossed anybody's mind that you are perfect, so why state the obvious?" When I hear a husband or wife in an estranged relationship say, "I know I'm not perfect," I want to say (but don't), "Okay, now that we've established the fact that you are not God, where do we go from here in figuring out what went wrong?"

One gorgeous summer evening, I somehow managed to get my five-year-old son to go out with me for a walk around the neighborhood. The air was balmy, the wind was pushing the trees back and forth with a great swooshing noise, and the stars looked like they had been sprinkled there just for us to delight in. I pointed upward. "Just look at all those stars, Christopher."

"I know what the stars are, Dad." He paused, then pronounced, "They are all of our sins that have gone away."

Now, at that moment I didn't know whether theological accuracy was the most important thing or affirmation of a genuinely spiritual idea coming, somewhat creatively, out of his five-year-old mind. So I just asked, "What is sin, Chris?"

With a bit of incredulity, he snapped back, "Well, *you* ought to know, Dad."

I said nothing, preferring to believe he knew that I had an advanced degree in theology, rather than that I was a particularly expert sinner. Wishful thinking, perhaps.

WE'RE ALL EXPERT SINNERS

The truth is I know I am a good sinner; it comes naturally for me. Nobody drags me kicking and screaming into envy. I don't need any particular inspiration to be impatient. I didn't need to take a seminar in covetousness to want things that don't belong to me. I say things that are careless and unkind, and I think things that are in direct contrast to the mind of God.

All of that would drive me to despair, except that this truth about my nature, and that of everybody else I know, fits right into the faith that I hold to. The whole scheme of Christian truth includes this sad but true piece: the ever-active sinfulness of the human race. And if you accept that premise, it's a lot easier to understand the nature of the world we live in. The good news is that Christian faith doesn't leave us there. God's work through his Spirit brings about purification from sin, a retraining of human nature based on the free forgiveness of God made possible by the voluntary death of Christ. Amazing! Incredible!

But let's stay a bit with the issue of sin, because we can't experience the full healing and redemption God offers if we don't understand the disease at work in us.

BREAKING UP WITH GOD

At its core, the meaning of sin is a break in our relationship with God. Sin is "anything in the creature which does not express, or which is contrary to, the holy character of the Creator" (Oliver Buswell); "the refusal to find our anchoring . . . in the holy love of God" (Hendrikus Berkhof); "lack of conformity to the moral law of God" (Louis Berkhof). Or, as my son put it, "*You* ought to know, Dad." And of course, we do. We all do, when we're honest, and we must be honest on this score; otherwise we will never rise above our sin.

The prophet Isaiah put it this way: "For our offenses are many in your sight, and our sins testify against us. Our offenses are ever with us, and we acknowledge our iniquities: rebellion and treachery against the LORD, turning our backs on our God, fomenting oppression and revolt, uttering lies our hearts have conceived" (Isa. 59:12–13). Notice the key to the lock here: *acknowledge.*

In one breath, the prophet lays out a glossary of sin (offense, iniquity, rebellion, treachery, oppression, revolt, lies), and he establishes that we sin in thought (what the heart conceives), word (lies), and deed (all the rest). "Thought, word, and deed" is a way of talking about the whole of our lives. It is a way of saying, "God, I need my whole life to be exposed to your healing touch. I need to be honest about my transgressions that are overt acts, those that are careless words, and those that are imaginings which spring from secret motives."

We can be thankful that sin, in its essence, is the negation of what is good. It is the *-less*, *un-*, or *dis-* of the created order: lovelessness, lawlessness, godlessness, thanklessness, faithlessness, unbelief, disobedience—in other words, darkness. Why be thankful about that? Because sin has no existence in and of itself. Go into a dark room and turn on a light, and the darkness disappears. "The darkness is passing and the true light is already shining" (1 John 2:8). I've met many people who feel utterly hopeless about their faults and transgressions. They feel terrible that they keep disappointing God, and they wonder whether anything will ever be different. And this is key: they view their mistakes as an essential part of who they are rather than as a good gone wrong.

Sin must be taken seriously. This disconnect from God is the universal condition of the human race, as Scripture makes abundantly clear: "There is no one who does not sin" (1 Kings 8:46); "No one living is righteous before you" (Ps. 143:2); "Who can say, 'I have kept my heart pure; I am clean and without sin'?" (Prov. 20:9); "The whole world is a prisoner of sin" (Gal. 3:22); "We all stumble in many ways. If anyone is never at fault in what he says, he is a perfect man, able to keep his whole body in check" (James 3:2); "If we claim to be without sin, we deceive ourselves and the truth is not in us" (1 John 1:8).

"I am not a perfect man." Well, yes.

Against these gray clouds and darkness that cover the human race stands one distinctive life—a brilliant, even blinding, light. Jesus the Messiah, called by many names, is also known uniquely as "him who had no sin" (2 Cor. 5:21). Because the glory of God shines directly from him, and because it is undiminished even by his true human nature, Jesus is the answer to the problem of sin. Darkness doesn't stand a chance against the light. And considering him who was called "the light of the world" and "the light that shines in the darkness," we have always before us a brilliantly illuminated life, the way human life was supposed to be.

But we also have to take the time to understand the seriousness of our plight without God.

DEAD OR ALIVE

This is how serious our plight is: the father who received back the prodigal son said, "He was dead and is alive again; he was lost and is found." It is one of Jesus' most beloved stories, the story of a son who snatched his inheritance and squandered it in reckless living. When he found himself eating with the pigs, he wondered if maybe his father would hire him as a manual laborer and trudged toward home. There he found a waiting father.

"He was dead." How else could we describe living life utterly separated from God? "You were dead in your transgressions and sins" (Eph. 2:1). That makes the forgiveness and love that come from God in Christ all the more remarkable. God "made us alive with Christ even when we were dead in transgressions" (Eph. 2:5). Jesus himself said that those who believe in him have "crossed over from death to life" (John 5:24).

Christian faith holds that the brokenness of our humanity has affected every faculty we possess. The heart is easily given to deceit (Jer. 17:9). The mind is darkened (Eph. 4:18). Even the conscience, that moral watchdog that is supposed to warn us when we stray, is corrupted (Titus 1:15). Does this mean that we are incapable of thinking good and doing good? No. Does it mean that our faculties are as corrupt as they can possibly be? No. Does it mean that every person sins in every way that is possible to sin? Obviously not.

Not everyone commits murder, or adultery, or theft. But it would be a major spiritual mistake to take refuge in the fact that we can always point to someone else who seems to be guilty of graver moral errors than we are.

Hitler's deeds make none of us angels by comparison.

Two things are true of every human being we share the planet with today: we all belong to a race created in the image of God, and we all have become broken, twisted, and corrupted. It's not that we are sinners because we commit sins; our brokenness is so universal and so constant that the only way of understanding it is that we sin because we are sinners.

Are all sins the same? Of course not. Murder is a distinctly worse offense than shoplifting. The commonality among us is not in the sameness of what we do wrong; it is in the status of belonging to a race of fallen, broken creatures. Jesus forgives criminals who seek his mercy as easily as he forgives people who cheat on their taxes, cheat on their spouses, or tend toward a bit of gossip.

MOUNTAINS AND CREVASSES

What is sin? "*You* ought to know, Dad." I guess I do know, because I know myself. But I also know that I need to keep this part of my faith, this belief in something we'd rather not believe, intact and more refined with the passing of time. As faith grows, so does our understanding of just how many ways we fall short. It is like driving closer and closer to a mountain range and seeing the peaks loom greater and higher but also seeing the crevasses and valleys more dramatically too. A secular vision of life offers a flattened landscape. No one is terribly bad and no one is spectacularly good. Give me real mountains and real crevasses any day, particularly because that is the way things really are.

Consider this scenario: Every day as Jack wrapped up his work and gathered his things to go home, he experienced a sinking feeling that he would give anything not to go home. He had felt this way before, when his first marriage had failed eight years earlier. This second marriage wasn't supposed to be like this. The heat of new-found passion was not supposed to fade away into iciness. He had thought he'd go on feeling that soothing sense of something exciting flowing through his veins when he was with her. But now it was just like the first marriage. In fact, he even had flashes of an unbelievable thought: Was I happier the first time around?

Worst of all, Jack was utterly confused because his second wife was accusing him of exactly the same things his first wife had. It was like being in an echo chamber. In the first marriage, it hadn't been hard to deflect the accusations by thinking, "I'm not self-centered; you are. I'm not neglecting you and the kids; I'm just providing for our needs, and I can't help it if I'm irritable at the end of the day. I wouldn't get so angry if you weren't such a witch."

For every accusation, Jack had a corresponding and neutralizing counteraccusation. Somehow that arithmetic had worked in his mind, and it was easier to leave his first marriage than to even consider that he might be at fault. But the refrain of the same accusations about his character and behavior in the second marriage was leading Jack to the edge of a frightening, even desperate, realization: "Maybe I am shutting people out of my life. Maybe I am a self-centered jerk. Maybe I don't have a clue." Looking in that mirror every day and having the same self-doubts was a terrifying experience.

Jack realized he was at a fork in the road. He could begin to admit to himself and to others that for all his success in external achievements, he was a miserable human being in so many ways, and he had, in fact, caused so much hurt. Or he could cut and run again. But run where? And would he find himself looking in that same mirror again?

"Confess your sins." That has to be the hardest thing God asks us to do. But if we can accept the diagnosis, we can receive the cure. Acknowledging that our lives are often like pieces lying on the ground gives us our best chance of the pieces being put back together.

PRAY THIS

Lord, it is hard for me to admit my mistakes and to confess my spiritual rebellion. I know I have hurt people by what I've said and by what I've left unsaid. I know that so many of my actions and my thoughts fall far short of what you hope from me. I also know that you would not speak to me about such things unless you wanted to lead me onto a better path in life. In my heart, that is what I want. Show me the next steps.

FOR REFLECTION OR DISCUSSION

1. What are some examples of brokenness caused by someone hurting or failing someone else?
2. One description of sin is darkness and ignorance. What real-life examples of this can you think of?
3. How do Jesus' words about crossing over from death to life strike you?
4. Which of the biblical passages cited in this chapter is particularly striking to you today? Why?
5. What are the most significant unanswered questions you have about sin?

WHY DO BAD THINGS HAPPEN TO INNOCENT PEOPLE?

And I asked why, why, why, oh God?
Why did it have to be only my sister who
was killed on the patrol that day?
— *Twenty-year-old American soldier,*
speaking at her twin sister's funeral

It is the mystery that always seems to move farther from our grasp the more we reach out for an answer. The question that makes us bristle when we hear it. The question we can't help but ask.

Why do bad things happen to innocent people?

Years ago I would have responded to this question differently than I do today. I assumed that it, like most questions, was a blank needing to be filled in, a query needing the most biblical and reasonable solution that can be offered. And while that is partly true, it's obvious that for many who voice these words, it is not a question at all. It is a cry of anguish. It is the way people say, "I am hurting so badly, and I just don't understand it." No matter what "answers" someone gives to the problems of pain and evil, suffering people are still left with an empty space in their lives that was once filled by what or whom they have lost. Answers don't replace people. The question is one not of philosophy but of personal need: "Why, oh why, does this have to be?" Or, as the psalms so often say, "How long, O Lord?"

I've been asked many times by someone in a severe crisis, "Why?" The blank expression, the lines etched deeply in the face, and the wide, searching eyes all echo the question. No matter what explanation I offer, the emptiness in the person's face doesn't disappear. It is like pouring water into a bucket with holes in it. The one thing that does seem to "take" is the truth that God is with us. And sometimes we are more aware of that when we are suffering than at any other time.

Driven toward God amid the Suffering

How can we explain that the people who suffer the most are usually driven not toward the black hole of skepticism but toward God? The parent who loses a child, the worker who loses a job, the young woman whose doctor tells her she has to come back for a biopsy— how frequently these people cry out to God in their distress, their pain taken not as proof that no one above is listening but as the occasion to believe all the more, to pray that most solemn of prayers: "Have mercy on me, O Lord."

Philip Yancey, in *Where Is God When It Hurts?*, quotes Scottish theologian James Stewart on this point: "It is the spectators, the people who are outside, looking at the tragedy, from whose ranks the skeptics come; it is not those who are actually in the arena and who know suffering from the inside. Indeed, the fact is that it is the world's greatest sufferers who have produced the most shining examples of unconquerable faith."

Simplistic Answers

Some people have looked for a commonsense, real-life kind of answer and have thus wondered, "Maybe God isn't good," or, "Maybe God isn't almighty." The first proposes that bad things happen simply because God can do whatever he wishes, and it just doesn't matter that it seems bad to us. The second is to say that God would like to prevent bad things from happening but he is just not able to do it; perhaps not even God is able to keep up with all the chaos in the world. If only God had one war to deal with at a time.

But most of us realize that to give up on God's goodness or his greatness is to believe in an utterly different kind of God. Not God at all, really. But this is not what Job or Jeremiah or David meant in the Old Testament when out of the pits of their distress they asked, "Aren't you good, O God?" In their most honest prayers (intentionally left in Holy Scripture so we can know that God would rather have us say anything than stay silent), these sufferers were simply saying, "We know, God, that the evil things that happen are so contradictory to who you are, such a violation of what you stand for; please reassure us that you are in fact the good God."

Another misleading solution is to simply believe that God does not exist. But atheism has always been, and always will be, a cheap answer. Augustine pointed out that if you ask, "If there is a God, why is there so much evil?" then you also have to ask, "If there is *no* God, why is there so much good?" Atheism solves nothing. It offers no comfort, takes away no pain, provides no hope. The only comfort it provides is an act of supposed resignation that says, "You should have known all along you are only dust. Forget God and the Genesis breath that turns dust into man."

Others have tried to suggest that maybe the solution to the problem of pain is that suffering is illusory. This approach deals with pain by saying we only think we experience pain. The religion founded by Mary Baker Eddy, Christian Science, teaches this. Yet Mrs. Eddy did die. The idea that suffering is an illusion flies in the face of common experience. Even if it is an illusion, the illusion hurts a lot. There is still a problem.

GOD'S GOODNESS AMID THE BAD

When I visited Esther in her tin shed in a Nairobi slum, I found myself talking to the person closest to Old Testament Job whom I'd ever met. I didn't know at that moment that she was within a couple of weeks of dying.

This slum on the east side of the city is a cluster of huts and sheds made with odd-shaped pieces of corrugated sheet metal or stacks of sharp black stones. Tens of thousands of people are crammed into this area. A meandering path takes you through the clusters of shacks, and you step over the trickling streams of putrid open sewers. Children stare as you walk past. Adults give you a glance and even a friendly greeting. My Kenyan host, Jane, who runs an amazing ministry of mercy for mothers with AIDS, led the way into the six-by-eight-foot shed that was the home of Esther and her daughter. Reclining on her bed, too thin and weak to do more than raise herself on one elbow, Esther greeted us with a smile. I sat on the corner of her daughter's bed near a couple of pots and an alcohol stove on the ground. Jane had Esther flip through the yellowed plastic pages of a small picture album, which brought smiles to Esther's face as she briefly identified who was in each picture. One photo was of Esther on her wedding day, a tall and strikingly beautiful woman wearing the cleanest white and beaming the whitest smile, standing outside in the Nairobi sunshine. It was hard to believe this was the same person lying emaciated in that shack. A few pages over was a photo taken looking straight down on her husband's wooden casket lowered halfway into his grave by men holding two ropes. He had contracted HIV and developed AIDS first. Esther contracted the disease from him. Mercifully, their daughter has tested negative for HIV.

Esther's arms were covered with sores. She blinked slowly and weakly; her voice was raspy. But she spoke of the good things with joy. I learned that even when she was quite sick, she had given her testimony in church and that she never gave up loving the Christian songs she had led her whole life. The women, like Jane, who helped her get good nutrition and who were genuine friends were visible signs of God's grace flowing amid the sewers. When she had been strong enough, Esther had worked with the other HIV mothers in a small warehouse, making beautiful rugs. Someone had helped her do something constructive while she still had strength, instead of just consigning her to the number of the cursed.

"Curse God and die!" Job's wife had told him when he was in a similar situation. Some people do give up faith. But untold numbers reach the extremes that Esther did and cling to God right to the last moment. Those who choose atheism relinquish the only hope we have when all other hope is gone.

SUFFERING CAUSED BY EVIL

When we look at Scripture, the overarching truth we find is this: suffering is not the way things were meant to be, but God is moving things toward redemption.

There are numerous sources of suffering in the world. Foremost is Satan's destructive intent—that malevolent evil force at work in the world. It's a voice that comes through the crafty serpent of Genesis 3: "Did God really say, 'You must not eat from any tree in the garden'?" Untold suffering has happened in the world because people have chosen to succumb to temptation, no matter what harm may come to others. In the story of Job, Satan says that he has been "roaming through the earth and going back and forth in it," the picture of a pure predator. The Bible teaches that there is an Evil One who has an interest in all human suffering. When the apostle Paul is talking about a "thorn in the flesh" that he had, which was most likely a physical impediment, he calls it a messenger of Satan. Paul asked God to take it away—a prayer that we are always permitted to pray. Three times he pleaded with God. And even this apostle, who knew more about the power of God and the reality of evil than most of us do, knew this pain might be taken away and might not. He came to believe that God was giving grace in many other ways and that God's power would be seen in his weakness.

That story can be told many times over. Some of the people with the strongest faith show that strength at the hour of their greatest weakness. That is why evil does not have the final word. Evil may delight in pain, but evil never cashes in on pain.

SUFFERING CAUSED BY HUMAN SINFULNESS

Another source of suffering is human sinfulness. The first murder occurred just four chapters into the Bible. What's worse is that it was a brother killing his own brother. Why did bad things happen to a shepherd named Abel? Because Cain chose hot, bitter jealousy. Cain had the opportunity to live in harmony with God, but he took his God-given ability to choose and listened to the dark side of his nature.

God doesn't murder; people do.

C. S. Lewis speculated that 80 percent of the world's suffering is caused by the immoral choices of human beings. Several years ago I was in the Ethiopian countryside looking over vast, fertile fields. The grain was laid like great sheets across the hills, shifting in color and shadow as it was pushed this way and that by the breezes. Women wearing red and yellow and green walked along the road, hunched over with large baskets on their backs. My guide told me that Ethiopia is fertile enough to feed the whole of Africa. I recalled the severe famine in Ethiopia in the 1980s. Although there was a drought in those days and the crops were affected, the real reason for the famine was sinful human beings who hoarded the available grain and prevented its distribution—purely political and tribal manipulation. *That* was why hundreds of thousands of people died in the famine. God did not cause people to shrivel up and die of malnutrition; cruel human beings did. And it is not the way things are supposed to be.

People naturally ask, "So why can't God prevent people from causing others to suffer?" The answer is that he could, and someday he will. He will decisively interrupt the affairs of the world and bring a curtain down on history; judgment will come, along with a new creation in which there will be no more tears and no more pain. But in the meantime, God allows human beings to exercise a quality that is one of the most noble things human beings possess, and also one of the most dangerous: freedom.

THE DIGNITY AND DANGER OF FREEDOM

Freedom is one of our most cherished attributes. Why did young men emerge from landing crafts on the beaches of Normandy and run up the beach in the face of leveling gunfire? Why did they throw themselves toward the vicious teeth of a powerful enemy? Why did they lay down their lives, many of them never to take another step toward age twenty? They did it for freedom, because we need to be free to live. To be human means to be free. That's the way God made us; it's the way things were meant to be.

But the very meaning of freedom is that we are free to choose good and we are free to choose evil. That is, in fact, the only way freedom works.

We experience this every day with our growing and developing children. If someone asked you, "So, when exactly did you lose control of your kids?" the right answer would be, "What makes you think I ever had control of them in the first place?" A parent realizes with the passing years that parenting is not about control but training. Even if you physically constrained a child, you would not really control him or her, because a human being, no matter what age, asserts the drive to act freely. He or she may outwardly comply, but crossed arms, knit brow, and stiffened lips reveal an independent will inside. Parents realize their teenagers are progressively moving toward independence. How could it be any other way? Teenagers will soon be adults and will have to make daily decisions on their own, which will come out of whatever ethical and moral fabric has developed in their consciousness. With freedom of choice, adolescents will make good decisions and bad decisions, and that will continue through every phase of life that follows.

To be human means to have freedom, whether we use it or abuse it. That doesn't mean we are uninfluenced by forces without and within. Free choice does not mean we are entirely self-determinative. We are profoundly influenced by God, by other people, by temptation, compulsion, and addiction. But in the end, only we are responsible for the choices we make.

Why do bad things happen to innocent people? Frequently it is because human beings act carelessly, cruelly, and maliciously toward each other. Which, of course, leaves us asking, why? Why must this be? Why would someone abandon a baby at a rest stop? Why would someone have his or her spouse murdered? Why would someone drive by a house and randomly fire a gun at it? Why would someone kill another person for a wallet or a jacket? Why would someone fly a jetliner full of innocent people into a skyscraper? There is no good answer, because there is nothing of goodness in any of these acts.

The question of why innocent people have to suffer because of such acts is, at its core, unanswerable because it is nonsensical. But even without a rational explanation for what is in essence irrational, this piece of reality does fit with everything else we know about reality. The foolish and dark use of freedom is a fracture in the world and can be traced from one end of the human race to the other; it runs to the heart of human nature. There is a terrible consistency in the randomness of this kind of suffering.

Could God have created humanity without the awesome power to choose? Yes, he could have, but then we would have been robots, not human beings. We would not know a single moment of *chosen* love or devotion or goodness. We would not be able to worship God or love our children or our friends. We would be incapable of understanding grace instead of greed, light instead of darkness.

God wanted to make a certain kind of creature as the last step of the creation. He created human beings and invested them with this incredible privilege and power, the life-giving and life-taking power of freedom. The misuse of freedom has set into human nature a series of fault lines that go not only through humanity but through the whole creation. Like us, the whole of creation groans "as in the pains of childbirth," is "subjected to frustration," and "waits in eager expectation" for God's final redemption, when the bondage will end and the adoption of sons and daughters of God will be complete (see Rom. 8:18–39).

SUFFERING—WHAT'S IT ALL FOR?

Why do bad things happen to innocent people? Is there any purpose in it all?

Here is where the issue stings. If I have to suffer, is it all for nothing? Must I pay such a high price for no apparent benefit? How can God expect me to lose—just lose?

The Bible teaches that there is indeed a higher purpose in suffering. But the way we get there is not by calling a bad thing good. We don't have to go through mental gymnastics to somehow call it a good thing when a car crash decapitates a teenager; or when cancer cells, which violate all the rules of how healthy cells are supposed to behave, invade a person's body; or when soldiers wipe out the women and children of a village. If we don't maintain the moral and spiritual acuity that sees evil for evil and good for good, we've entered a confusing fog.

God is almighty, and good is what it is, just as evil is what it is. But here is the hope: God works through the bad, bringing us inexorably to a better place. How could it be any other way? He is a God of construction and repair, of putting pieces together and putting pieces back together.

We should never blithely tell someone who is in the middle of the agony of their suffering that "it is all for the good." But when the time is right, we can say with sensitivity that the God who is always good is never absent or indifferent. He holds all the pieces of our lives together in a whole that can never be calculated as a negative but is always a positive.

I have lived forty-five of my forty-nine years without a father. I can count dozens of times when I thought it would have been so good to have a father: to watch a football game I was in, to show me how to shave, to meet my fiancé, to introduce me to his friends at the shop, to ride with me as I learned how to drive. I had thought that grieving the loss of my father would have occurred in the first few years after his death, when, in fact, every new phase of life brings an awareness of the missing element in the equation, of the empty space. Yet the loss somehow does not tally up as a negative.

God's Different Kind of Algebra

In reality there are no set equations in life; God works a different kind of algebra. If one seemingly essential part of life is torn out, life does not collapse.

My father's death meant that I grew up in Wisconsin instead of Illinois, with an extended family who came around me like a safety net. I saw life from the perspective of a town of two hundred instead of a city of five million, enjoying regular exploratory trips to the town dump and twice-a-day swims in Lake Michigan. Later we moved to Green Bay, Wisconsin, and lived two miles from the stadium during the days of coach Vince Lombardi, when professional football players were the town's heroes and were friends you saw at the department store. I figured out how to shave *and* how to have a styptic pencil close at hand. The empty space was never very empty—only empty of one specific person.

I'm certain that growing up fast, having to be the man of the house while still a boy, taught me a sense of sober responsibility in life. It trained me to be a leader, although that was the last thing on my mind, especially after suffering a withering defeat in my run for class president in high school at the hands of a pothead who benefited from a three-way split.

I live daily with a sense of my own mortality, which I take to be a good thing. And I've had dozens of opportunities to talk to young families who have lost their mom or dad and let them know that even though it seems like they've lost everything, they've lost some-*one* but they're not alone.

Although losing my father at age four is a significant loss, I cannot imagine the losses some people endure—people wearing tattered clothes in a refugee camp, people who are physically or sexually abused by a parent or priest, people with chronic severe pain, the multitudes who never have enough to eat on any day, people who are unjustly imprisoned. Yet I hear the personal testimony of so many who have suffered so much and who have seen the math and still believe that the sum of life is positive. This is not to say that if they were to write the bad things in one column and the good things in a second column, the second would be longer than the first. It's more mysterious than that. Somehow God is able to keep the heart beating, the spiritual breath flowing. He brings light into even the darkest corners.

That is the promise we hold on to: "In all things God works for the good of those who love him" (Rom. 8:28). Not that all things are good (they're not). Not that all things add up to a positive sum (life is not about accounting). Not that all things become good things (that's just not true). Rather, God is at work amid "all things," which means every day and every chapter of life, even the dark ones. He is at work. He doesn't sleep, and he doesn't leave. Any work that God does is good, because he is God.

That is why "the Spirit helps us in our weakness" (Rom. 8:26), why we can believe "our present sufferings are not worth comparing with the glory that will be revealed in us" (8:18), why we can live knowing that "if God is for us, who can be against us? He who did not spare his own Son, but gave him up for us all—how will he not also, along with him, graciously give us all things?" (8:31–32).

Why do bad things happen to innocent people? There really are no innocent people. We're all good creations that have been twisted, and we live in a spectacular world that also twists and turns and breaks into pieces every day. We use our freedom for good, and we choose to use our freedom in ways that spin us out of control. When there is order, when we are receptive and obedient, we see great things happen. When there is chaos, people get hurt.

But through it all, God remains the creator of good things and Lord and Master over all humanity, even when we so often choose bad things.

Today I received the news that a friend's eighty-seven-year-old father died, having suffered a major stroke a few days ago. He had been a pastor for sixty-six years and had seen his share of joy and sorrow. When asked what he thought about the suffering in the world, his reply was an old poem he had committed to memory. It is a simple confession, but those usually serve as our bottom line. It is a statement of what faith says when it looks at pieces and discerns God's redemptive patterns instead:

> My life is but a weaving
> Between my Lord and me,
> I cannot choose the colors
> He worketh steadily.

Oftimes he weaveth sorrow,
And I in foolish pride
Forget he sees the upper
And I, the underside.

Not til the loom is silent
And the shuttle cease to fly
Shall God unroll the canvas
And explain the reason why.

The dark threads are as needful
In the Weaver's skillful hand
As the threads of gold and silver
In the pattern he has planned.

PRAY THIS

God, there are many things that are hard for me to understand, and one of them is the hard times and sufferings that we go through, especially when we have not brought them on ourselves. Help me to trust in your goodness and to know that nothing that happens in this world changes your goodness. Help me to understand your distress over evil and to know that bad things do not compromise your goodness. When I am going through dark days, help me to persevere until the light dawns again. I pray for people I know right now who need to be aware of your steady presence because of the battles they are going through.

FOR REFLECTION OR DISCUSSION

1. Who do you know who has asked, "Why do bad things happen to good people?" Under what circumstances?
2. When have you asked that question?
3. What situations do you know of in which someone found God's grace in the midst and in the aftermath of pain?
4. How can we use our God-given freedom for good rather than for evil?

WHO AM I REALLY?

4

My soul is my greatest asset
and my greatest misfortune.
— *D. H. Lawrence*

If someone were to ask you, "Who are you, really?" a complete answer would have to include something about the invisible you, the part within that is different from the body. One of the truest things you can say about human beings is that they are so much more than meets the eye.

Yet we play to the eye.

OUTWARD SELF VERSUS INWARD SELF

Think of someone you know who, by most people's standards, is extraordinarily handsome or beautiful, a picture of health, possessing a vivacity that turns people's heads, but who is empty on the inside.

At thirty-six years old, Marilyn Monroe, sought for the best movie roles and the most popular magazine covers and one of the best-known female icons of the twentieth century, took an overdose of pills to end her life. By becoming larger than life, almost revered as a goddess, she lost her inner self, and she put the icon in the grave.

The outward self can profoundly contradict the inward self.

At the other extreme is Hector, that droopy old man you might see sitting on a park bench feeding the pigeons every day. Clothes from Salvation Army, folds of skin hanging off his face and neck like a bloodhound, wart on his eyebrow with one big hair coming off it because he hasn't had a chance to get to the doctor to have it taken off. And why would he? It's just part of who he is. But Hector is at peace. He put in his thirty years at the factory, gets by on his monthly checks, goes to church regularly, and has very few moments of doubt about his identity as a human being.

WE ARE MORE THAN THE SUM OF OUR PARTS

The belief that we as human beings are nothing more than chemical factories changing oxygen and food into energy day after day until the factory breaks down and we die is extraordinarily hard to maintain, but not for lack of trying. Many philosophies and religions limit themselves to the certainties of what we can touch and measure—things such as fingers and eyeballs and the amazing network of nerve fibers in the body. Proponents of this idea say, "Listen to common sense; what you can see is all there is. It's all there ever will be. The sum total of a man or a woman is what can be placed on a scale or in a coffin." Yet, like a great hot-air balloon that refuses to do anything but ascend, the idea that we are more than our bodies, that we have a soul, that we're not done when we're dead, keeps rising in most people's convictions.

Despite sociological and anthropological theories about why we think we have a soul, the simplest explanation, of course, is that there really is a soul, just as when you hear music coming from a house with an open window, you assume that some source of music lies inside the house.

We shouldn't think for a moment that the soul is an issue only for the dark oak hallways of philosophers; it is every person's issue. The question "Is there anyone home in there?" will determine how I treat other people today, how I will act when I get in a disagreement with my spouse, how I will respond if the doctor tells me they have found something suspicious and need to run more tests.

Let's say you meet Person A, whom you like right from the start. You're intrigued by what you see in Person A, but you know you have to withhold judgment because superficial contact doesn't really tell you much. It is by talking, by sharing views about the world around you, by speaking of yourself and drawing out the other person, that you gradually develop a relationship. And let's say you then see in this person someone whom you could spend a lifetime with. Now the stakes have been raised considerably. Now you really need to know what kind of a person Person A is. But you won't know that until you hear the mind of Person A more fully or until you see the heart of Person A responding to joyful or painful circumstances.

Whenever I officiate at a wedding, standing right between bride and groom, I always wonder, "Do they know, really know, the person it is they are marrying?" Of course, some do, quite well. They've invested time with each other. They've talked about matters that go far beyond wedding preparations; their preengagement interactions and courtship were not just maneuvers for a nuptial bid. They've shared their hopes, fears, dreams, biases, failures, successes, joys, and humiliations. They stand there not as animated gowns and tuxedos flanked by misty-eyed bridesmaids and fidgety groomsmen; they are persons who know they are joining themselves to another person.

Our Mask, Our Self

Our word *person* comes from the Latin *persona*, which means "mask." Not a negative idea, *mask* refers to a public presentation of self. Because we are persons, we are always communicating who we are, and we have to do the work of understanding the person sitting across the table. And so we "read faces." We look at people's eyes as "windows to the soul."

In the English language, *soul* is shorthand for the inner self, which is understood in vastly different ways. Lord Byron made this comment: "One certainly has a soul, but how it came to be enclosed in a body is more than I can imagine." Henry Wadsworth Longfellow wrote:

> Tell me not, in mournful numbers,
> Life is but an empty dream!
> For the soul is dead that slumbers,
> And things are not what they seem.
> Life is real! Life is earnest!
> And the grave is not its goal;
> Dust thou art; to dust returnest,
> Was not spoken of the soul.

The Bible gives us detailed insights on who we are on the inside and how we function as thinking, feeling, willing creatures. It all begins with the wholeness of the person. However much we distinguish the parts of a human being, the Bible assumes that a person is a whole thing. A unity, not pieces. So you don't come to worship bringing your emotions with you (on the assumption that religious things are purely a matter of sentiment) but leaving your mind in the lobby and your body back in bed (although I know some who would like to send their spirits to church so their bodies can stay under the covers). No, worship is an intentional act that is intellectual, emotional, and even physical—vocal chords vibrate with praise, tongues taste the bread and the wine, and bodies feel the cleansing water of baptism.

The unity of our visible and invisible selves is why public officials and others in the public eye cannot say that what they do in the intellectual arena can be divorced from what they do with their bodies, any more than a burglar could stand before a judge and say, "It's my body that's at fault, not me."

ONE PERSON

We are body and soul—one person, with two major aspects: the external (visible, fleshy, sensory) and the internal (thoughtful, moral, volitional). Throughout our lives, these two aspects are inseparable. Our spiritual reactions come from the experiences we have with what we see, hear, smell, taste, and touch. A husband loves his wife well when he does it with devoted thoughtfulness, emotional understanding, and physical touch. God's greatest command is that we love him with heart, mind, soul, and strength.

The relation of our visible and invisible selves is like the relation of house and home. *House* refers to the physical building, whereas *home*, though not separate from the house, points to the greater spiritual reality, a living thing. You repair a house, but you live at home.

There is that unique moment when the spiritual self is separated from the bodily self—when the last breath is exhaled and, like Jesus, we can pray, "Into your hands I commit my spirit." It is then that our "earthly tent" is destroyed and we go from being "at home in the body" to being "away from it" (2 Cor. 5:1, 9). How can we ever comprehend this as long as we are creatures of the earth? None of the stories of spirits haunting houses and ships, or even having friendly exchanges, are truthful or helpful. What the Gospels teach is that Jesus told the thief on the cross, "Today you will be with me in paradise," and Paul said he knew that if he had to be "away from the body," he would be "at home with the Lord."

DYNAMICS OF THE INNER LIFE

So there is one person, with two aspects, but also with many functions. Here is where we get a refined view of who we really are. The rich biblical vocabulary about human nature describes the dynamics of our inner life as being made in the image of God. Some passages describe our inner functions, and others emphasize a truth about what we are like.

The biblical word *mind* refers to the inner life, especially emphasizing our rational, cognitive, intellectual capabilities (Rom. 7:25; Col. 2:18). *Heart* (Rom. 10:6–10, for instance) refers to the deep inner core of our lives, where opinions and beliefs are formed, where we sense right and wrong, and where our love is centered. The Bible's use of *heart* is inclusive of thought, emotion, and will, unlike the English use, which often refers only to emotion. Just look for the word *heart* in some of the psalms sometime, and you will see how Scripture points us to the core so that we will understand the deep place where our very selves are shaped. *Will* refers to the faculty of choice (Luke 22:42), and *spirit* is used to describe how human beings, unlike dogs and cats, salamanders and oak trees, are persons, made in the image of God, possessing morality, consciousness, creativity, and other godlike characteristics. And *soul* refers to the human person animated by the living power of God.

None of these are "parts" of the human being. We can no more separate human nature into different components than we can view the attributes of God as the constituent parts of his being.

THIS IS WHO I AM

So if someone were to ask you, "Who are you, really?" a biblical answer would be, "I am part of God's creation, and I belong to a species that was uniquely shaped to bear the likeness of God. That is why I have a sense of ought and ought not and why I hope to grow in selfless love. That is why I am able to speak to others, why I imagine things that could be, and why I worship. I am a creature made of clay. I have a body that processes thousands of responses and reactions every hour but that is also easily injured and made sick. One day this body will again become the dust of which it was made. But I am also spirit and soul. Inside my body is a self-conscious, self-willing spiritual center. At this heart of myself, I am constantly combining the thoughts that come to me from the outside, the voice of God's Spirit speaking to me, and the things I'm telling myself. But mixed in there are also selfish and wicked motives that come from the inner spiritual fractures I was born with and are amplified by external temptations."

The biblical answer is *not* that I am a spirit trapped in a body, and one day when that body dies, my true self will be liberated to coalesce with the eternal Spirit. Those who have believed this over the centuries have thought that the spiritual self is the only true self, and the body, like the rest of the physical universe, is a mass of troublesome dirt. This view holds that our spirits are sparks separated from the divine fire, that we bear in ourselves a bit of divinity. It also negates the value of God's creation of physical things.

No, I am not destined to become a ghost. Nor will I discover one day that I was God all along.

Nor is the soul, as others have proposed, a dreamy combination of commonly held feelings, thoughts, images, symbols, and memories that have produced the merely cultural phenomena of religions, myths, fantasies, and fairy tales. This view sees human beings as animals that have very vivid dreams and like to share them with each other.

No, the Bible depicts us as creatures almost too good to be true. And that makes the reality of sin and wickedness in our thoughts and deeds the greatest tragedy the world has ever seen.

GOD'S BREATH IN US

When I finished college, I took a third-shift job working as a nursing assistant in a nursing home. My wife, who was training as a social worker, suggested that one of the best ways I could prepare to be a pastor is to take care of people who are in their most vulnerable time in life. And she was right. In the months I spent working from 11 p.m. to 7 a.m., watching over a ward of elderly patients through the dark and unquiet hours of the night, I learned so much about our physical frailty, the unexpected cry in the middle of the night, and the endurance of the soul.

One night the head nurse told me that a ninety-year-old lady who had bumped her head and whose vital signs were very unsteady would probably not make it through the night. She had no family nearby, and so would I be willing to sit with her during her final hours?

In the darkened room, all I could focus on was the unevenness of her breaths. Short, panting, long, stopped. A couple of times she stopped breathing, and when I stood up, she started again, almost as if the sound of my shuffling feet stirred her back. But finally, when the last erratic breaths came, followed by one long exhale with a gutteral groan (the way I had heard a lot of people relinquish their last breath), the bedsheets lying across her chest and abdomen sunk lower than before and then were absolutely still. Total silence and total peace. It was almost as if her breath was her living soul, and when it left the room, it was like a person walking right out the door. As we lifted her into a body bag, it was obvious from the flaccidness of every muscle that there was no life there, none whatsoever.

When he breathed his last breath, Jesus said, "Father, into your hands I commit my spirit." The Hebrew and the Greek words for *breath* can also be translated as "spirit" or "wind." So breath is the most obvious symbol of life itself, especially of that inner animating principle the Bible calls *soul*. It all began in Genesis: God formed the man from the dust of the ground and breathed into his nostrils the breath of life, and man became a living soul.

So if you are reading this, it means your last breath has not come, and your spirit or soul is still animating your body. The pieces of personhood are still together, and you have an extraordinary opportunity to glorify God with what you do in heart, soul, strength, mind, and body in the days you still have. But you have to believe that these pieces of your life—body and soul, thought and emotion and will, creativity and morality—all hold together, making you a member of the most complex and sophisticated race God ever made. The pieces of what makes you you may seem like a puzzle sometimes, but they all come together to form a picture that God held in his mind long before you were ever born.

Pray This

Dear God, you have said that the most important thing is that I love you with all my heart, soul, strength, and mind. Help me to learn what that means. Help me to seek you with my mind and to have a sense of awe at the truth of who you are. Help me make right choices with the remarkable will you gave me. Help me to honor you by what I do with my body. Work in me, at the center, at the heart, where even now my ideas and opinions and passions are forming before I am even aware of them.

FOR REFLECTION OR DISCUSSION

1. How many different words can you think of that describe the inner life of human beings?
2. What aspects of your inner life are you most comfortable with? What aspects are you least comfortable with?
3. What evidence do you think there is that we are more than animals?
4. Consider some of the verses in the psalms that use the word *heart*. What does Scripture say goes on at the core of our being?
5. How is our everyday conduct affected if we believe that we are spiritual creatures with God-created minds, hearts, wills, spirits, and souls?

IMAGE IS EVERYTHING

5

What a chimera, then, is man!
What a novelty, what a monster, what
a chaos, what a subject of contradiction,
what a prodigy! A judge of all things,
feeble worm of the earth, depository
of the truth, a sink of uncertainty and error,
the glory and the shame of the universe!
— *Blaise Pascal*

Press a button, and the television screen brightens. What was a dead, gray screen now projects a cool-blue background, a multicolored logo in the lower right corner, and a head-and-shoulders shot of a newscaster whose skin shows no blemish, whose hair is sculpted, whose voice flows, and whose eyes lock on your own. How could you not listen to such an image, though in truth it consists only of alternating points of light and two dimensions?

THE ALLURE OF IMAGE

One of the outstanding features of the modern era is that the power of image has been harnessed as a new religion. Image is power, control, and allure. Aspiring to have a good image is the new version of the quest for holiness. But if you live by image, you will die by image. The sculptors of image today present us with a continually rotating gallery of pictures of perfection. But if they snatch our allegiance and our longing, they will also leave us disappointed and defeated. We will never attain that image of perfection, and chasing after it will leave us exhausted. We will have no meaningful understanding of imperfection. Wrinkles will demoralize us because we will see them as the irreparable scars of time instead of as the marks of maturity and credibility.

I do not know who first coined the phrase "Image is everything," but whoever it was captured the spirit of the contemporary world about as well as can be done. People in the public eye—politicians, entertainers, civic leaders, novelists, sometimes even spiritual leaders—often work desperately to shape and polish a public persona that will please the most people. We ordinary people pick up the cues. But are we all supposed to be images pleasing to some external eye?

IMAGE REALLY *IS* EVERYTHING!

Here is the truth of the matter: image really *is* everything. But the image that matters is a moral form, a spiritual shape; that is the manner of the way we were created.

"Then God said, 'Let us make man in our image, in our likeness. . . .' So God created man in his own image, in the image of God he created him; male and female he created them" (Gen. 1:26–27). Here, just twenty-seven verses into the Bible, is a manifesto on all of life, based on one basic reality about humanity, one unique characteristic: we are images of a greater being.

You get up in the morning, you look in the mirror, and reality hits. Blemish, blemish, stubble. Tousled hair, sticky eyes, foul breath. (What a great image!) Then you shrug your shoulders, step away, and walk out into this day in your world. Or do you?

This is the comical point of the epistle of James when it says, "Anyone who listens to the word but does not do what it says is like a man who looks at his face in a mirror and, after looking at himself, goes away and immediately forgets what he looks like" (James 1:23–24).

The implication is not "Go back to the mirror, man! Peer at yourself, clean yourself up, make that image sparkle!" No, James goes on to say, "But the man who looks intently into the perfect law that gives freedom ... will be blessed in what he does" (v. 25). It's not about the size of the mirror or how long you stand in front of it. It's about which mirror is worth using in the first place.

In other words, if you want a real look in the mirror, a true image of who you are, who you could be, and who you are meant to be, then don't be like Narcissus, who was enamored with his own image in the mirrorlike pool.

In this Greek story, Narcissus was an irresistibly handsome young man. When he was born, his mother was warned that he must not look at himself, so she hid all the mirrors that were in the house. As he grew, everyone told him what a handsome person he was, and he began to think of himself as something special. Women fell in love with him, they threw themselves at him, but no one was good enough for him. But one day as he was hunting, he fell to his knees in front of a glassy pool of water to get a drink and immediately fell in love with the image he saw there—his own. As he gazed into that pool, he became captivated with himself, but for all his shouts and reaching out, the image gave no response, and Narcissus died there of a broken heart.

James has a better alternative: look at the mirror of God's Word, for that is where you will find a true image of who you are to be.

No twenty-first-century image consultant would ever think to say that you were created in God's image, in his likeness. But to find your true self, you should not just look inside yourself; the key to what is inside you is actually found outside you. You didn't just develop; you were made, shaped by the hand of the master clay-shaper, knit together in your mother's womb. God, who made you, is the reality of which we are just an image, a likeness. Image really *is* everything. An old man whose face is full of bumps and canyons may have a better self-image than a beauty whose face is smooth as a platter of milk—if it's God's image.

Genesis, as the revelation of beginnings, says that only humanity is made in God's image, nothing else—not horses, not flamingos, not kangaroos. Scientists tell us that the DNA of chimpanzees and humans are remarkably similar, but you just won't see a chimpanzee performing Mozart in a concert hall or designing a submarine or going to worship. So what are those things that can be said only of human beings and God, and not of anything else in all creation?

We Are Moral

For one thing, God is *moral*, and so we are (which, of course, means we are capable of moral understanding and action, not that we always do it). Only human beings have the noble thought of "ought." Yes, your dog may have learned not to relieve himself on the carpet in the house because he knows he'll be locked up in his kennel if he does, but this is primitive conditioning, hardly a thing we'd call conscience. Right and wrong. Just and unjust. Fair and unfair. Pure and impure. Proper and perverse. Murder is wrong for one reason alone: the image (Gen. 9:6). Unless a person has stiffened his conscience into complete insensitivity, seared it shut, killed it dead, he will still sense that there can be found a bold black line between ought and ought not. And for all the efforts of some in the contemporary world to make us believe that these impulses are merely the arbitrary tracings of social convention, we can still point to the soul-centered joy and satisfaction that we experience when we see the right done. Morality cannot be silenced. Morality will make all but the most darkened soul glad.

Morality is not wimpishness but an exuberant shout. Morality is not narrow-mindedness but big-heartedness. It is not a club to beat you up or to be used by you to beat others up. It is, instead, freedom—a break from a chaotic prison where it is every man for himself and the only law is force and muscle.

We Are Creative

For another thing, God is *creative*, and so are we. Now, only God brings nonexistent things into existence. Only he creates something out of nothing. But he apparently has passed on to us at least the ability to dream dreams that have never been dreamed before, to design buildings that have never been conceived before, to make a machine that will leave the orbit of the Earth. Only from the human race has come the hanging gardens of Babylon, *Romeo and Juliet*, the Coliseum of Rome, the *Mona Lisa*, and the U.S. Constitution. And that places human beings closer to God than any other creature. You will never find a robin returning to your backyard and deciding this spring not to make the same boring round nest but a duplex instead. Or a square nest. Or a nest made of mud instead of straw. No, the robin can only follow the innate instructions of its imprinted nature; it is extraordinarily uncreative. But we must remember that creativity is not in itself holy. Clever minds have also dreamed up the nightmares of the Tower of Babel, the rack, and the hydrogen bomb. Even the godlike qualities we possess can be used for demonic ends if separated from the power and purposes of God.

WE ARE SPIRITUAL

Then there is *spirituality*. God is *spirit*, and he created humans to be *spiritual* beings. Have you ever seen an animal seeking God? Now, the cynics of the world may think that shows just how wise the animals are, that they know better than to be religious. But we know that we can do better than living merely as animals. You will never go to your kitchen in the early morning to find your cat or dog having a time of morning devotion. You will find no spiritual journal. Nobody has ever or will ever find in the deep, dark forest a religious shrine that the woodland animals constructed in their search for communion with God. Whale song, yes, but whale hymns?

For all the beauty of the natural world and the spectacular nature of its creatures, for all the evidence of divine theme and variation, complexity and simplicity, God did one more thing when he created humanity. He said, "Let us make this one in our image."

GOD RESTORES THE SHATTERED IMAGE

I was moving a floor-length mirror once and dropped it on a concrete floor. Hearing that shattering, and seeing the silvery shards spread across the floor, is an awful sensation. And, of course, the old canard about seven years of bad luck leapt to mind. Maybe that superstition has some symbolic meaning, because when you bend down to look in a broken mirror, you see a grotesquely splintered image. All pieces, nothing whole.

This is the way many of our days go. We try to get a good view of things, an accurate image of ourselves, but because the mirror is lying in pieces, we get a shattered image. It's no use trying to glue the mirror back together. Even if you could, the least skewing of the pieces would produce a disjointed and disturbing image.

That is why God needed to restore the image, which he did in one great saving act. The Son became the Savior and, as the likeness of God, draws us to a different kind of mirror, one in which we see and are shaped by his transforming image. That is why when we read the Gospels, we find ourselves awed by a Jesus who is larger than our lives will ever be but who is also truly like us. Have you ever been angered at hypocrites, heartbroken at a friend's graveside, exhausted by the demands of people, frustrated by a lack of understanding in your family or among your friends? That's Jesus. That's us. Peter even thought that maybe he could walk on water like Jesus. As it turned out, the water was no problem, but a gap in faith was. Jesus is the perfect image of the true God and the true image of perfect humanity—a mirror without flaw.

Over the years I've heard so many heart-wrenching stories of people who lived for years under the domination of someone who continually attacked their personhood. Through demeaning speech and out-and-out lies, these people prey on others in an attempt to bring them down or to bring them into submission. They leave people with a mirror that is like the twisted and bent mirrors you find at a carnival or like the shattered mirror on the ground.

But I've also seen these victims healed. They see the dirty or bent or broken mirror for what it is, and they ask God for a new one. It can be a challenge to stick with the new mirror instead of looking back at the old. It may even be threatening. But they come to know that they are better off with the truth than with a deception.

Image is everything—especially when it is the true one.

Pray This

Dear God, I know I cannot live with an image of myself that I have dreamed up or that others have invented. I need to know reality. I want to see myself as you see me, even though I know that means seeing my blemishes as well as the glory that you put there. Please bring into my life people who will be honest with me. And please, when I read the Bible, let me find those truths that will open my eyes wide and that will shine a bright and revealing light on who I am and what the world around me is. Help me to see things the way you know they can be.

For Reflection or Discussion

1. What are some examples of how are we tempted in the world today to play the game of image making?
2. What disappointments have you experienced or witnessed in the quest for a publicly acceptable image?
3. What has happened in your life that has caused the mirror to crack or shatter?
4. What aspect of Christlikeness would you like to pray for God to produce in your life at this time?

Part 2

God Puts
the Pieces Back
Together

PROVIDENCE

6

*I shall never believe that
God plays dice with the world.*
— Albert Einstein

As I write this, it is the first day of January, and I find myself wondering what this new year will bring. One more trip around the sun: 8,760 hours. Last year, most of those hours turned out as I expected. But a few thousand did not. That's where the excitement comes in—and the worry.

LOOKING BEHIND, LOOKING AHEAD

On many coins and city gates of the old Roman Empire appears a bearded figure with two faces poised in opposite directions. This was Janus, the god of gates and doorways, and the god of beginnings. A new beginning is a doorway of sorts, a marker that you have moved from one spot in life to the next. And so the first month of the year, January, is named for this figure who looks one way to the past and the opposite to the future. Why is it important for us to have a perspective on what has passed? The best way to enter the new is with a considered awareness of the old.

How might the year ahead unfold? Or this month, or even this week? I can speculate about opportunities and challenges, pleasures and pains, but I just don't know what this next piece of future will bring. And I'm sure it's a good thing I don't.

Only God knows the future and, more important, is the caretaker and Lord of the future. One bedrock truth of the Christian faith enables believers to move into the future with assurance: providence. More than the idea of a deity with two faces who looks ahead and behind, the biblical God is above all reality, encompassing in his vision and embracing in his power past, present, and future. God purchases no calendars, keeps no schedule on a PDA, develops no project charts. He is never surprised by what happens but is alternately pleased and displeased by what does happen. God takes us toward a good future, pointing us toward a life goal that no human being would have conceived. The good path is always just the next few steps in the direction of the good end.

PROVIDENCE: GOD'S ONGOING GOVERNANCE

Providence is the ongoing activity of God in preserving and governing everything he made. It is exactly what you would expect of a Creator whose work of creating is an act of love. How could he possibly act indifferently to his creation, which he bestowed such care on at the start of it all? He not only put the pieces of the universe together when it was created, but he is still putting pieces together and putting broken pieces back together. Providence is care that precedes and care that proceeds. It is the benevolent attitude of God toward what he has created. God respects what he has done.

Some people have a hard time believing in any form of providence. They may acknowledge a creator or designer, but one who is now no longer directly involved in the creation. They don't see a gigantic hand reaching down from the clouds; they believe that most of what happens in life can be traced to natural cause and effect. God may be a watchmaker who produced an impressive machine, but now those gears and springs are clicking through their motions on their own. Science yields real knowledge, while theology and spirituality offer only sentiment. One page of the calendar flips to the next, and the events of our days are just the random collisions of our lives with each other, a time line of the collection and loss of goods. This belief yields a religion that seems sensible and nicely under our control. God is in the far corner of the universe; he's done what he does best, and now we get to be the center of the action. We are left, like children whose parents have gone away on a permanent vacation, with a few moral guidelines and a lot of latitude.

But the biblical testimony allows no such benign view of God. It shows God to be enthusiastically involved in protecting and guiding those he has made. Why would he be a watchmaker? How would that in any way be consistent with a character of active love and intense, creative interest? The watchmaker analogy works only for those who have decided that it's easier to understand the world if it is no more than moving parts, a piece with pieces, and that's that. But can you take a walk in the woods or camp alongside the ocean or fly over the countryside or watch a meteor shower and think of the universe as a watch?

The watchmaker analogy has been used because it serves our desire to say, "I prefer to think of you as removed from my sphere of influence, God. Thank you very much for creating, but now it's time for us to take over, to be at the top of the pyramid of all things. So it's fine if you stay in your seat in the corner of the universe; don't feel as though you need to get up on our account. Frankly, it's easier to calculate things if we don't need to figure you into the equation."

But this is God's world. The biblical vision is that we live with expectancy and confidence through faith in his ever-close activity. Providence is the basis for hope for the future, the reason we can go from dark December, through the festival of light and life marking the birth of Jesus, and on through the doorway to a new year in January. Providence says that a year isn't just one loop around the sun; it is a forward journey along a time line which God stands simultaneously at the start and end of, and at every point in between.

Someone said that it is as if God were viewing a parade, but not as we do, standing in one place, watching each event pass us. Rather, God's perspective is similar to that of a man standing on a tall building, simultaneously viewing the parade at its start, middle, and end.

The band in the middle of the parade has a definite past (that spot where two of the trumpet players fainted) and an anticipated future (are those kids ahead holding water balloons?). But the man on top of the building sees everything, all at once.

Providence comes from a Latin word meaning "to foresee." God looks ahead, in other words. His vision is like the wheels ringed with eyes that move to and fro in the visions of the Old Testament prophet Ezekiel. God's eyes are not like the spots on a pair of dice that turn randomly up and around and over. This day is more than the breathless hope that the dice will come up in our favor, only to watch them be thrown again tomorrow. The only people who think it's okay to look at life as just a big gamble are those who have not done very much gambling.

DO NOT WORRY ABOUT YOUR LIFE

Here's a word from Jesus' Sermon on the Mount that we would do well to ponder within the first waking hour of every day: "Therefore I tell you, do not worry about your life, what you will eat or drink; or about your body, what you will wear." It doesn't get any more practical than that. In the Sermon on the Mount, Jesus made some of the preeminent statements in Scripture about the providence of God. He was addressing one of the pressing questions we all ask: Who is going to take care of me? On your eightieth birthday, that question might have a special urgency, but in truth it is no less urgent when one is twenty.

The answer? "Your heavenly Father knows you need them," so don't get caught in the rat race or, as we might say, the pagan chase ("the pagans run after all these things" [Matt. 6:32]). There is a better alternative, in other words, to living a life of hoarding. As someone said, the problem with the rat race is that even if you win, you're still a rat. Our security does not come from the bank statement, telling us how much we've saved up, or from the number of suits in the closet. Food in the pantry is a good thing. But no matter how much we have to eat or drink or wear or drive or shelve, we will never know security until we see the face of providence: the God who clothes the lilies of the field and who tends to the birds of the air. And he knows. He knows what we have and what we need. He knows those days when we have less than we think we need, too.

Sparrows fly, but they also fall. But not one of them falls to the ground apart from the will of the Father (Matt. 10:29). This year may be a time for us to feed and fly and travel far, or it may be the year of a broken wing or that final plummet. And that is where providence figures in more powerfully than anywhere else.

The facts of pain and loss and even overt evil do not nullify the reality of providence. While we try to explain the dark, the greater reality will always be the light. The only reasonable explanation for the way things work is that the Creator of all things keeps it all going day by day.

A thousand things could go wrong with my body right now, but at the moment it seems to be working just fine. My breakfast is being converted from fuel to energy, and the oxygen my lungs are sucking in is making bluish blood turn red and rich. My brain is sending thousands of commands a second, and my heart muscle is relentlessly contracting like a fist, pushing lifeblood to every external and internal cell. I'm not amazed that I can so easily get sick or injured. I'm astonished that my body works as well as it does. And there is only one explanation: continual divine care.

Both times my wife was pregnant, I tracked over the months the progressive extension of her midsection—the most spectacular thing I've ever seen. From the outside, it just looked like swelling, then bulging, then amazing protruding. The whole affair seemed more than human. And, of course, it was.

But hearts don't always work right, and sooner or later they all stop. Some pregnancies end in miscarriage. At this moment there are at least a dozen wars going on in the world. Crimes are being committed against property and person, and unspeakable things are going on behind closed doors. But the incidents in which things don't work well are set against the backdrop of so many healthy days and good relationships and proper exchanges. Generosity, forgiveness, forbearance, support, patience, kindness: these are among the many gifts given every day. And there is only one explanation for this: divine governance.

The proof of providence is the fact that it never stops raining permanently, living things keep growing, and the human race keeps reaching out for hope and life. In so many ways, the creation keeps asserting itself. It is irrepressibly alive, even though pieces of it keep dying. But more importantly, the Creator keeps asserting himself. God keeps saying, "I've made what I've made. And I will keep it going and growing, and re-create when I need to."

> He who dwells in the shelter of the Most High
>   will rest in the shadow of the Almighty....
>
> He will cover you with his feathers,
>   and under his wings you will find refuge;
>   his faithfulness will be your shield and rampart.
> You will not fear the terror of night,
>   nor the arrow that flies by day,
> nor the pestilence that stalks in darkness,
>   nor the plague that destroys by midday.
>   —Psalm 91:1, 4–6

These words from Psalm 91 are echoed many times throughout the Old and New Testaments, and not by people whose lives were easy. Those who suffered hunger and persecution, tyranny and anarchy, betrayal and abandonment—those are the people who spoke of their undying faith that God really does care for and govern all things, despite the belief of petty lords that they have the upper hand. Despite the fact that sparrows do fall.

PROVIDENCE AND THE PATTERN OF GOD'S CHARACTER

Providence is true because of God's character. It is his nature that defines his relationship with everything that he made. The piece of your faith that says God is good lines up with the piece that says that life is divinely superintended. Living theology begins with God and then takes you on a tour of the rest of reality. God's nature and acts are the landscape from which all other things grow.

To put it more personally, Jesus said in the Sermon on the Mount to go ahead and ask God, seek God, knock on his door. He is the Father in heaven. We see in the pattern of earthly fathers—when they are behaving the way fathers should—that they don't give stones for bread or snakes for fishes. No, fathers don't do that, and "your Father in heaven gives good gifts."

You might think that people who have very little would have a more difficult time believing in providence than those who have much. But I find that the more I have, the easier it is to forget about providence. If there is plenty of food in the pantry, lots of clothes in the closet, and money in the bank, I'm tempted to trust in the provision rather than in the provider. And when I trust in the provision, I worry about whether the provisions will run out. How much is enough? Well, just a little bit more.

But how does that farmer in Mexico with a small plot he has worked by hand year after year trust that he will have what he needs? He has no choice but to keep on planting and keep on praying. Because he has known times of drought, he understands the harvest, and he receives it as the blessing of heaven. He does not presume what he cannot assume. He is able to trust, and he is able to exercise patience as only a farmer comprehends patience.

I don't know exactly what February will bring, or April, October, November, or December. I suppose it's likely that next January I will be on this planet having looped millions of miles around the sun, and the billions of people with me will have had countless interactions. We will have seen the seasons come and go. We'll know someone new and say goodbye to someone we've known for a long time. We'll see.

But this much we can know: God will not change. His loving care for his creation will not stop. No nation will challenge his governance and succeed. And nothing will happen outside his vision.

Believing in providence, that God is governing what he created, gives us peace of mind because we live in a piecemeal world, and we need to know that our benevolent Creator is holding the pieces together. Heaven does touch earth. God's plan for the world is not lost in the newspaper headlines of the world. The broken pieces of our lives are actually the building blocks with which God rebuilds our lives. The only things that are torn down and remain rubble are the things that cannot (and should not) be rebuilt. Everything that is eternally good will be on display in the new heaven and the new earth.

Pray This

Dear God, help me to have the faith of a farmer. Help me to be joyful for the rain and deeply gladdened by every mealtime when there is bread on my table and for every night when I can lay my head down and slow my breath into a night of rest. Keep me always in awe of your active work in this world. I am grateful for the rhythms of life, but I also believe that you still do the miraculous. If you choose to point me to you in a new way through a special act, I pray that you would keep my eyes open to it.

For Reflection or Discussion

1. A traditional Christmas carol speaks of "the hopes and fears of all the years." What are your hopes and fears for the days that lay ahead of you?
2. The same carol goes on to say that those hopes and fears "are met in thee [Christ] tonight." What do you need to do now to link your hopes to Christ and place your fears in his hands?
3. In what ways do you need to "dwell in the shelter of the Most High" at this point in your life?

GOD UNCOVERED

7

When I was young, I said to God, God,
tell me the mystery of the universe.
But God answered, that knowledge is for
me alone. So I said, God, tell me the
mystery of the peanut. Then God said, well,
George, that's more nearly your size.
— *George Washington Carver*

I felt so ignorant the first day of political science class in college because I knew nothing about the subject. The first day of sociology class was the same. I couldn't even spell *sociology*. And it was particularly true of pottery class, where the lean, tousled-haired professor wearing denim from top to bottom mumbled through his opening speech about how he was going to teach us to make art from cold lumps of gray clay. I knew my hands were not those of an artist, and I couldn't imagine how the class would change that.

I don't like feeling ignorant, so I am tempted to avoid situations in which my ignorance is revealed—which is, of course, a very ignorant thing to do.

If you feel ignorant enough and then experience new knowledge seeping in, then flowing in, you realize it's no shame to be ignorant. It simply means you don't know, and thus you are in a perfect position to be a learner—a disciple. If you don't know, one of the smartest things you can say is, "I don't know," because the best way to ensure that you will never know is by keeping the doorways of your mind, heart, and spirit closed or by being too self-conscious about someone poking around inside and hearing a little echo there.

I don't know how many times I've heard someone say, "I'm afraid to speak up or ask a question because I'm afraid of looking stupid." What a shame we do this to each other.

Just stop and think of what God can do when we intentionally take the posture of the unknowing and say to him, "Teach me what I do not know; show me what I do not see; lead me where I am not going; reveal to me what is concealed behind the veil."

How Can We Know God?

How can we mortals say we can know God? There is only one answer: revelation. Belief begins with unbelief (or spiritual ignorance), and then out of the darkness comes the light of God. Out of the silence, his Word. We can know God only because he wants to be known and makes himself known.

John Calvin's *The Institutes of the Christian Religion* is a landmark work in the history of Christian thought, and it begins with these simple words: "Nearly all the wisdom we possess, that is to say, true and sound wisdom, consists of two parts: the knowledge of God and of ourselves. But, while joined by many bonds, which one precedes and brings forth the other is not easy to discern." Calvin was saying that we have a drive to understand ourselves—our origins, our purpose, our physiology, our psychology, our spirituality—and this leads us to want to know God because we are made in his image. Then, as we try to know God, we are carried along to a deeper understanding of ourselves. This process leads to revelations such as, "Oh, I am to be truthful like *that*, and faithful like *that*, merciful like *that*." Understand God and understand yourself. Understand yourself rightly and better understand God. And so the cycle goes.

KNOWING GOD FROM THE EARTH UP

But how can we know God? Is it from earth up? Or from heaven down? Many honest truth seekers believe that the evidence we have about God and his whole realm of truth is written on the earthy tablets of nature and human experience. If you want to know what it means to be human, then study a multitude of samples of the creature, make observations about their customs and physiology and relationships, and draw your conclusions about what it means to be human. What you believe about humanity is the cumulative analysis of what you experience with a great many human beings. Collect your data; draw the inferences.

Do the same thing for God: look for the traces of his being, the signs of his character written in the stars and the patterns in nature and in human consciousness, and draw your conclusions about what God must be like.

This earth-up approach is the way we know about most of the ordinary things in life that we are curious about. It is how scientists diagnose and treat disease, how mothers figure out if their babies have ear infections, and how boyfriends learn to read the nonverbal signals sent from their girlfriends (for which there is no known reliable textbook). It is the way of knowing by generalizing from the particular. Theoretically, our knowing becomes clearer and more refined as we gather an ever-wider body of experience.

KNOWING GOD FROM HEAVEN DOWN—REVELATION

But there is an alternative way of knowing. The heaven-down approach is very different. This is the way of revelation. It does not negate the earth-up way of knowing, at least when it comes to knowing about very earthy kinds of things. But when it comes to knowing God, a different kind of knowing is required. A dog can sniff around a person's footprints left in the soil, but that doesn't amount to any real knowledge of the person. We may be able to pick up certain generalities about God from our experience, but it takes the voice of God, the uncovering of himself, to really know him.

Revelation is God himself speaking loudly and clearly about who he is and how he views the world; it is our responsibility to listen clearly. He speaks because he wants to be known. Imagine that—he *wants* to be known. A god who is just an energy force in the universe has no such desire, in fact, has no desire at all; an impersonal deity is uninteresting in the extreme because it is uninterested. If there were many gods, maybe a million or more, there's not much of a chance that one god would have the desire to be known by the human race, and even if he or she or it did, would we really care?

But a personal and infinite God knows and relates, and so he speaks—and speaks clearly. We need to make sure we are listening, not as astronomers do with the massive radio telescope dishes that sweep the sky listening for a faint pulse in the universe. If those scientists did hear the faintest sign that there was some intelligent life out in space, it would be revolutionary. Even finding a fossil on Mars—which has no intelligence, no knowledge, and no voice—would generate massive enthusiasm. It would be deemed another Copernican revolution. So when believers appear to be stunned with delight that a message has come from the greatest being in the universe—not one message but thousands of messages—nobody should be surprised that they become fanatically spiritual. What else is the appropriate reaction to beholding what God himself slowly and deliberately uncovers?

Skeptics think that if there is a God, he must be deaf and mute, because God is not broadcasting on the frequency they are tuned in to. But who should determine the frequency, the greater being or the lesser? Should we really focus on why God chose one frequency over another, instead of just being awestruck by the fact that messages from the Creator are coming through?

GOD *HAS* SPOKEN: SPECIAL AND GENERAL REVELATION

The biblical view is that God *has* spoken—through his chosen representatives, the prophets and apostles, and preeminently, through his Son, Jesus Christ. These are God's chosen frequencies for broadcasting his truth. This is revelation, and it is a different manner of speaking than any we are used to.

The *special revelation* that God gives us includes Jesus Christ himself, the Word that was from the beginning and was with God and was God. Jesus put it this way: "If you have seen me, you have seen the Father." The other major example of special revelation is the word of God in Scripture, the living testimony of truth given through people with the special calling of prophets and apostles. This is the way the book of Hebrews puts it: "In the past God spoke to our forefathers through the prophets at many times and in various ways, but in these last days he has spoken to us by his Son, whom he appointed heir of all things, and through whom he made the universe" (Heb. 1:1–2).

The salient points are simple: God is real. God has spoken. We must listen.

We could philosophize about who God could be and settle on the alternatives that seem most reasonable, but if God has spoken in the revealed word and in the Word made flesh, then doesn't all other knowledge about him move to the margins of the page? The fingerprints of God may be evident in a spiral galaxy, in the wildflower petals of an Indian paintbrush, and in the spiritual impulses that we experience, but what are fingerprints compared to voice and face? Give me the galaxies, for sure, but I will be able to know and adore and love a God who actually speaks.

God has also given us *general revelation*, which the apostle Paul talks about in Romans when he writes, "Since the creation of the world God's invisible qualities—his eternal power and divine nature—have been clearly seen, being understood from what has been made" (Rom. 1:20). These and other biblical passages say that we as human beings have plenty of evidence that God exists and that he is powerful and superlative and beautiful as designer of the universe. But apparently this is not enough. Human beings easily turn away from the mere fingerprints of God with indifference. A fingerprint doesn't call out to you, it can't lead your life, and it does not embrace you when you need to be comforted.

So God spoke. He revealed. He pulled back the curtain, uncovering what was shrouded (in the Bible, *revelation* means "an uncovering"). He spoke from heaven (that is, from his realm of existence), not by taking us up a ladder to heaven but by extending heaven to earth in the person of Jesus. Martin Luther was adamant that our belief be based on a "theology of the cross." That is, we know God not by ascending to where he is but by looking upon the one who has come to where we are. The Messiah's message was loudest when he was lifted up on the wooden post. We know God when we know the crucified Jesus.

This is the God who wants us to know him. A cancer patient can know God best through the suffering Jesus. So can a rejected spouse, an orphaned child, a discouraged pastor, an unemployed factory worker, an ashamed addict, a remorseful thief, a convicted felon, a teenage mom.

Just ask them. They want to know a God who is "familiar with suffering," even "despised" and "rejected" (Isa. 53:3). Because God is revealed in the suffering Jesus, we can know God at the times in life when we most need to know him. And so can any of us, at any time in life, under any circumstances. This is what the Bible means by the scandal of the cross. Proud human beings typically shun suffering as weakness, but God said, "I will meet you at the crossroads of suffering. At a place of blood, you will know me as the sacrificing God that I am."

His voice has gone out. Through Christ and in Scripture, a detailed record of truth has been etched deeply into the history of God and humanity. Now God does the work of revealing to us the true character of that revelation. God the Holy Spirit works in the center of our lives to shape this knowledge of God. The Holy Spirit inspired prophets and apostles, and now the Holy Spirit illumines us. That is the point of 1 Corinthians 2:7–14:

> We speak of God's secret wisdom, a wisdom that has been hidden and that God destined for our glory before time began. . . . God has revealed it to us by his Spirit.

The Spirit searches all things, even the deep things of God. For who among men knows the thoughts of a man except the man's spirit within him? In the same way no one knows the thoughts of God except the Spirit of God. We have not received the spirit of the world but the Spirit who is from God, that we may understand what God has freely given us. This is what we speak, not in words taught us by human wisdom but in words taught by the Spirit, expressing spiritual truths in spiritual words. The man without the Spirit does not accept the things that come from the Spirit of God, for they are foolishness to him, and he cannot understand them, because they are spiritually discerned.

How can we know God? We know him from his heaven-down revelation, which he continues to explain by his Spirit to every individual believer who wants to learn "spiritual truths in spiritual words."

Why should we know God? When God pulls the cover off any part of reality, speaking about our true nature, our purpose and destiny, our problems, our connections with the world and with him—whatever the issue is—we should snap to attention, alert to the lesson of the day, because God is the only one who can explain it all and give us a network, a grand pattern of truth. He speaks because he loves. He fills our ignorance not just with truths about him but with himself.

What does it matter if we know God or not? Some people liken knowing God to taking an elective class in school. Different strokes for different folks. Some people are into physics (but not everyone), some are into political science (but not everyone), and some are into God (but certainly not everyone). But knowing God has never been reserved for a special class of people—the kind who wear black robes or who are abstract-minded. Knowing God is more like a child knowing a parent. It's not an option; it's the way to live.

"And we pray this in order that you may life *a life worthy* of the Lord and may please him in every way: bearing fruit in every good work, *growing in the knowledge of God*" (Col. 1:10, italics mine).

PRAY THIS

> *Dear God, I believe that I can spend my lifetime getting to know you and still only just begin to understand who you are. I believe that because you are a God of love and grace, and because you chose to create me, that you want us to know you. Help me to understand what you have said to us through the prophets and apostles. Help me to know you through Jesus, and especially to know you through the merciful act of your death and the power of your resurrection.*

FOR REFLECTION OR DISCUSSION

1. What examples can you give of general revelation, the ways in which people look around them and see general evidences of God and of his character?
2. How do people respond in different ways to general revelation?
3. What aspects of the special revelation of God—Christ the Word and Scripture as God's word—have been most arresting and compelling in your life? In other words, what parts of God's revelation have affected your life the most?
4. As you look more closely at 1 Corinthians 2:7–14, can you come up with examples of how you learned "the thoughts of God" or "spiritual truths" only through the work of the Spirit in your mind and heart?

GOD IS GREAT

8

If there were no God,
there would be no Atheists.
— *G. K. Chesterton*

God is great;
God is good;
and we thank him for our food.
Amen.

I must have spoken those simple words hundreds of times at the dinner table when I was a child, but I most certainly did not understand what they meant. Not really.

I liked the certainty in the cadence of the words. They marched out of my mouth, and as I ended with a pointed "A-men!" the deed was done, the prayer complete. Time to eat. When I wasn't troubling over the fact that "good" and "food" only rhymed with my eye, not my ear, I think I took some satisfaction in having said something that seemed very important about God. Often the most important things you can say about God come in a single word.

Great. And good. That is what God is like. That is who God is.

The so-called attributes of God are a way of gathering and synthesizing the biblical descriptions of God in the interest of knowing God as he really is. One way to summarize the attributes of God is to use two categories: greatness (attributes of God's being) and goodness (attributes of God's morality). The first describes who God is and the second describes what he does because of who he is. God's greatness is about his ascendancy over this world, over the universe, over all reality. Greatness is about his being eternal, all-powerful, all-knowing, and other qualities that we will never fully comprehend. Goodness, on the other hand, is about his relational qualities, which we know by revelations such as "God is love" and "God is holy" and "God is right." Many of these qualities were also imprinted on our spiritual DNA when God created us. He wants us to possess these traits because we are made in his image.

GOD IS MORE THAN HIS ATTRIBUTES

Before we go any farther, we need to be aware of some pitfalls to avoid. Listing all the attributes of God does not constitute a complete knowledge of God, like one understands an engine by looking at an exploded diagram and parts list on a blueprint. God's attributes are not separable pieces; God is not composite. He is more than the sum of his attributes. God's character transcends our descriptions of his attributes, and the Bible often describes God by saying not what he is but what he is not (for instance, he is infinite—not finite).

So it should come as no surprise that the revelation of God that comes to us through the Bible is wrapped in the history and real-life stories of hundreds of people across a span of thousands of years, written in three different languages, and drawn from several cultures. The diversity in the Bible is not contradiction but a gallery of encounters with God. It took all that for us to get enough portraits of God so that we could begin to know him appropriately.

God, the divine person, discloses himself to mortal persons. His descriptions are voice to ear, epiphany after thunder, and heaven to earth, as when God disclosed himself to Moses, who was hiding in the cleft of a rock: "The LORD, the LORD, the compassionate and gracious God, slow to anger, abounding in love and faithfulness, maintaining love to thousands, and forgiving wickedness, rebellion and sin" (Ex. 34:6–7).

Psalm 95:3 says, "The LORD is the great God, the great King above all gods." God is not merely greater than other powers. His is a difference of kind, not degree. He defines greatness and majesty. So, then, what are the attributes of God's greatness? (In the next chapter we'll consider the attributes of God's goodness.)

GOD IS SPIRIT

Jesus said that because God is spirit, his worshipers must worship in spirit and in truth (John 4:23–24). But what does "spirit" mean? Both the Hebrew word for spirit (*ruach*) and the Greek word (*pneuma*) can mean "breath," "wind," or "spirit." Like the invisible wind that comes from one direction then another and can assert itself with mighty power, so God comes as Spirit. Breath, too, is invisible, yet with breath, you are a living being; without it, you are dead. So "spirit" is a wonderfully precise description of who God is—"the King eternal, immortal, *invisible*, the only God" (1 Tim. 1:17, italics mine).

We all know that there are two fundamentally different ways of looking at reality. One assumes that only what can be seen, touched, tasted, smelled, or heard is real. This is the materialist position. The other view allows that there are realities beyond our senses, the metaphysical beyond the physical. It assumes that there is a divine Spirit who is not limited by the material world as we are. He moves as he wishes; he is actively present in all places at once. He comes to us as pleasantly as a breeze but also as a mighty cyclone.

If you put a negative spin on it, God's spirituality may seem like an inferior trait, as if he is less than the creatures and things we daily see, touch, and smell. It may seem easier to ignore God because he is invisible and to go on with occasional debates about whether God exists or not—which is like talking about someone who is, in fact, still in the room with us. If there were a lion in the room, we wouldn't ignore it, but it's not hard to disregard an invisible God.

But God's invisibility is not some lack on his part. It is what you would expect of a God who presides over a universe in which there are not just three dimensions but at least eleven, at last count, according to some physicists. And if someone says, "Why doesn't God just show himself?" the answer has to be, "He did!" "The Word became flesh and made his dwelling among us."

GOD IS AND GOD IS ALIVE

How can we summarize what God means when he tells us he simply is? When Moses asked God his name (for there were many alternative names for gods), God's answer was, "I AM WHO I AM." This was not a typical name such as "god of thunder" or "lord of water and earth" but was the simplest, most essential title.

God is. That is the essence of who he is. Before anything else existed—before mountains or horses or angels, before even matter itself—God was. He is the one unalterable reality. So we can worship him anytime, anywhere.

He exists not as an impersonal energy in the universe but as the living God. "The Father has life in himself" (John 5:26). No one brought God to life. He is the one living being who had no birth, and so he is the Father of all that is born. Moses, Joshua, David, Isaiah, and other voices in the Old Testament drew people's attention again and again to "the living God." This is what made him different from the other gods whose statues sat on shelves. The Old Testament prophets spared no sarcasm in talking about false gods who, because they were not alive, could not be life-giving. Isaiah depicts a man cutting a tree, using some of the wood to warm himself, and "from the rest he makes a god, his idol; he bows down to it and worships. He prays to it and says, 'Save me; you are my god'" (Isa. 44:17). Biting sarcasm! Elsewhere Isaiah talks about a man who looks for wood that will not rot before his god is carved. Scandalous! "He looks for a skilled craftsman to set up an idol that will not topple" (Isa. 40:20). (Hard to respect a god that keeps tipping over. Do you bend your head if he's leaning one way or the other? And if he topples over, wouldn't that suggest that you might fall no matter how strong your allegiance to this deity?) Hosea said the people "consult a wooden idol and are answered by a stick of wood" (Hos. 4:12). Just how many intelligent comments have you heard from a hunk of wood lately? And so in the New Testament, the apostle Paul commended one group of believers as those who "turned to God from idols to serve the living and true God" (1 Thess. 1:9), because if one thing is true about idols, it is that they are the most lifeless, ridiculous objects on the face of the earth.

Those of us who have no wooden statues on the hearth, however, are no less capable of idolatry. Whenever we make up an idea of God to suit our purposes, we are idolators. The same is true when we put something or someone above God as the determinative influence in our lives.

The only kind of God worth worshiping is a living God. A God who is living and all-powerful is completely outside of our control. What other kind of God could exercise authority and control over our enemies?

The only kind of God who could bring everything into existence is a God who "is" before anything else "is." He is Being before all other beings, including human beings.

No matter how clever and sophisticated any human-invented deity may be, no matter how refined the rites and rituals associated with it, no matter how erudite the philosophy that is attached to it, the one thing a human-invented deity cannot be is divine. But the true God can, and did, invent humanity. Whether we acknowledge it or not, we are all God's offspring.

A few weeks ago I was approached by a bright, young ninth grader named Carly who invited me to her high school auditorium to hear her give a speech to her class on the subject "The special person in my life is . . ." For this assignment, most of the students had chosen to speak about a sister or brother or parent or friend, but Carly had asked permission, first from her teacher and then from the principal, for her speech to be "The special person in my life is God." It was an offer I couldn't refuse. But only as I heard Carly unfold her personal story did I understand the full import of this seven-minute speech. I didn't know until then that Carly is deaf and had been listening to my messages in church for years by reading my lips. I also didn't know that when she was born fifteen years ago her physical impairments were extreme: cleft palette, hole in her heart, abdominal irregularities. She did not have the ability to swallow, so for the first nine years of her life she lived off a feeding tube. For the first seven years, she needed the assistance of a respirator, and she suffered from seizures from the time she was four. In the first few years of her life, she was treated at Milwaukee Children's Hospital one hundred times and had twenty-five surgeries.

She had also endured ridicule from mean-spirited kids, especially in junior high school. Animals were her friends when human friends were hard to come by, dogs and horses especially. Her speech had a simple message: through it all, she was sustained by God's grace. The grace was incarnate in her parents, caring doctors, and friends.

When Carly said, "The special person in my life is God," she was not just saying that she had survived her first extremely difficult fifteen years of life; rather, she was saying that the Divine Person was with her actively, benevolently, and responsively. The personal God did what only persons can do—know another, love deeply, and serve as a powerful presence—even during long weeks in hospital rooms. And this gutsy little kid, who could have waited until her senior year to take speech class, jumped in as a freshman and gave glory to her "special person."

God of Abraham, God of Isaac, God of Jacob, God of Carly.

God Knows

Because God is personal, he is a knowing being. His mind perceives truth and defines truth. He embraces us with a knowledge that is not just stored information in a divine file but is an extension of love. His knowledge holds us.

> O Lord, you have searched me
>   and you know me.
> You know when I sit and when I rise;
>   you perceive my thoughts from afar.

You discern my going out and my lying down;
    you are familiar with all my ways.
Before a word is on my tongue
    you know it completely, O LORD.
You hem me in—behind and before;
    you have laid your hand upon me.
Such knowledge is too wonderful for me,
    too lofty for me to attain.
—PSALM 139:1–6

Psalm 147:5 says God's "understanding has no limit." "Nothing in all creation is hidden from God's sight" (Heb. 4:13). When you pray, you can be assured that "your Father knows what you need before you ask him" (Matt. 6:8). He knows the number of hairs on your head. He knows you better than you know yourself. God's omniscience is our comfort.

Because God's all-knowing character is an extension of his personality, the Bible is not a mystery book of hidden secrets, and ministers of the gospel of Christ are not soothsayers or crystal-ball gazers. The knowledge presented in God's Word is about the way things have been, about the way things are, and about the way things will be—as they must be—depending on how we respond to God's direction. Christianity is not a horoscope with saints' names attached. It is a way of life and a view of the world as it was, is, and will be. Many things that God knows remain secrets or mysteries to us. But many other things are uncovered, especially the consequences of the weighty spiritual and moral decisions we make every day.

GOD IS INFINITE

Have you found that the longer you live, the more you realize your own finitude? Perhaps you used to think you could accomplish anything, but you've grown to realize you can do what God has enabled you to do and what your own fragile mind and body will allow you to do. You can't be in two places at once. You can't make everybody happy. You can't get treatment for every disease, and you can't be twenty years old again if you've passed that mark. These are not bad things. They are just results of a quality that we properly and wisely accept: finitude.

We live in bodies that keep us located in one spot at one time. Our bodies break, they disintegrate, they fall to pieces. We know only so much, and the more we learn, the more we realize how much we do not know. Our knowledge leaks out of these holey buckets we call minds. We can build impressive machines, but we are virtually powerless before a tornado or the surges of the ocean.

In every way that we are finite, God is infinite. God is all-knowing (omniscient). He doesn't grow older, doesn't become mentally limited, doesn't show emotional fragility. His power (omnipotence) exceeds that massive energy that holds all matter together. God is present at all times in all places (omnipresence). "'Am I only a God nearby, . . . and not a God far away? Can anyone hide in secret places so that I cannot see him? . . . Do I not fill heaven and earth?' declares the LORD" (Jer. 23:23–24). When the Hebrews built a spectacular temple in honor of God, wise king Solomon dedicated it by confessing that even that divinely initiated place would not "locate" God. "The heavens, even the highest heaven, cannot contain you. How much less this temple I have built!" (1 Kings 8:27).

Omniscience, omnipotence, omnipresence. God is God in ways that could be true only of an absolute God. The implications for prayer and our dependence on God are enormous. Our prayers do not inform God of facts he is ignorant of. Rather, our prayers are an engaging conversation in which *we* wait to learn something *we* didn't know before, or in which we simply receive the comfort of talking to the God who knows our needs before we even ask him (as Jesus put it in the Sermon on the Mount). Because we pray to an all-powerful God, it is not the prayer itself that has power, but God. So we should be careful in talking about the "power of prayer." It is not our vocalizations that accomplish anything, and certainly we should never see prayer as some kind of incantation. The power comes when we open ourselves to the all-powerful God, when we become more fully aware of how God stands in the midst of our circumstances, a giant who cannot be ignored, who is never afraid, and who elicits proper fear in people. Omnipresence means that prayer is as effective when offered in your car as when offered in your church, whether in garbled words or moaning or crying. Prayer requires no antenna pointed in just the right direction at the right time.

Because God is great, something powerful is already at work the moment we say, "Dear God . . ." Even if the only thing we can say is "Dear God."

GOD IS CHANGELESS

Imagine our confusion if we thought that God is glorious (sometimes) or is Spirit (once in a while) or knows us (well, at least 75 percent of us, plus or minus 5 percent). No, whatever God is, he is consistently. God "does not change like shifting shadows" (James 1:17). Everything else in life changes. God will one day roll up the universe like a robe, "but you [God] remain the same, and your years will never end" (Heb. 1:12).

What a parent hopes to be—consistent, even-handed, fair, reliable, steady—God is. He always is. He is the only father who is never arbitrary, never capricious, never moody. What was true about God four thousand years ago when he called Abram is still true of him today. And so what is true about him today will be true for your great-grandchildren and for all eternity.

God is great. This is the song sung by the universe. It is the proper interpretation of every heartbeat, every breath, and every step of our lives.

This is what Mary, the mother of Jesus, meant when she said, "My soul magnifies the Lord." The news of God's act of supreme greatness, bringing a rescuer into the world, inspired her to praise and adoration. But Mary magnified the Lord not in the sense that she made him bigger but in the sense that her soul was enlarged by the greatness she was just beginning to comprehend.

No telescope ever made a celestial body larger, but by gaining a larger vision, a magnified vision, the beholder is changed by the greatness beheld.

God's greatness is our best hope to know that there is a way to pull it all together when we feel like our lives are just so many pieces. We are pulled together and held together by the greater purpose of a greater being. So when we wonder where we fit in, or how we can go on after losing somebody important, or whether we can do any good in our lives, the answer comes from the throne of the God of greatness. His invisible hand moves us more powerfully and carefully than any other influence in our lives. He is not puzzled by the puzzling pieces of life.

PRAY THIS

> *God, enlarge me. I don't ask you to make me bigger or more important, but I know that if I get a fuller experience of your greatness, my heart and my mind will be greater for it. But most of all, help me to be exuberant in setting a course of life to know your greatness and to speak of your greatness whenever I have the opportunity.*

FOR REFLECTION OR DISCUSSION

1. How can you better focus on God's glory through worship and prayer so that the weight of it makes its impression on you?
2. How has God's invisibility been either a comfort or a struggle in your mind?
3. Have you been thinking of God as a person or as a force?
4. What does God know about you that no one else knows?
5. In what ways can we be glad God is infinite?

GOD IS GOOD

9

God is good, all the time.
All the time, God is good.
 — *African proverb*

What if you believed in a God who wielded immense power, who knew absolutely everything, and who was not limited by time or space—in other words, a truly great God—but you had no assurance that he was good?

It is frightening even to imagine. This would suggest a God who acts by whim, who may be biased, and who is as likely to torture as to grace. He might alternate between being the benefactor and the bully of the universe. Yet this is the way many people think about God. They take all that is not good in the world and attribute it to God, and in this crude spiritual equation, God must end up the despot.

When one looks at the descriptions of God in the Bible, his true attributes, one finds a great God who is also good beyond measure. This goodness is described for us vividly and concretely with words such as holiness, righteousness, justice, love, mercy, grace, and truth.

HOLINESS

"Holy, holy, holy is the LORD Almighty; the whole earth is full of his glory." Those were the words the prophet Isaiah heard during his vision of God exalted, seated on a throne, the train of his robe filling the temple (Isa. 6:1–4). *Holy* means "separate, different, unique," and this is one of the best assurances we have that God is interested only in the good. He is separate from all the evil and malice in the world—not ignorant of it, but neither is he defiled or influenced by it.

God made a bold and clear statement about his holy character long ago in the Old Testament. All those laws, for instance, were God's way of setting aside one tribe in the human race for something different, a sure signal that any of us can be elevated to a different life. The children of Abraham learned over centuries about the holiness of God through the object lessons of the holy temple, holy basins, holy garments, holy days, and holy Sabbath. But they also were learning about love. Why else would God want any of us to learn of his holiness if not because, out of his deep love, he longs for us to know that life can be different? Relationships can be right. Decisions can be just. All the laws about what the Israelites could eat and wear, how they should sacrifice, and the holy time they should reserve for God's special purposes all pointed toward a single truth: God is unique.

One of our basic problems as human beings is that we tend to feel uncomfortable around what is different. One of the occupational hazards of being a pastor is that when people in the public sphere find out that you're "one of them," they sometimes get uneasy about you. A local shop was repairing my car earlier this week, and when the workers heard from their supervisor that I was a pastor, I overheard one say to the other, "Stop swearing; God is here." Another time I was at a football game and was seated next to someone from our church. When they greeted me as "Pastor," four people sitting in front of me turned to look to see if one of "them" was actually sitting behind them. For the rest of the game, the wife jabbed her husband in the ribs when he blurted out an expletive. I've gotten the weak handshake, the avoidant eyes, and the halted conversation. It isn't because these people don't like pastors (well, I tell myself that, anyway); they just don't like feeling different, and they assume you're different as a pastor.

So what is it like for God? Sometimes we run to God because he is holy and we know that the only hope we have in this world is a God who is so different from the world that he is our lifeline out of the chaos. But our instincts often cause us to shrink back from the holy God. For some people, it means a lifetime of avoiding him. Whether we realize how desperately we need him or not, we often consider it too risky to approach a God who is *that* different. So we may shrink from the holiness of God, but we should also long to live in his holy presence, because we all know that we need something and someone truly different from the vulgarities of this world. What other hope do we have that things can be different from what they are?

RIGHTEOUSNESS AND JUSTICE

God is right in everything he is and does. His goodness, in other words, is the shape of the way he relates to others. God has never done anything that is not right and will never do anything that is not right. Justice is God's rightness—his righteousness—applied in matters of judgment. In the final judgment, God will do what is right, and in the everyday flow of decisions, deliberations, and minor judgments, God's opinion is unfailingly right and thus good. Probably none of us fully realize just how much we need the judgment of God. Life presents us with puzzles. The pieces lie before us—all the complex factors going into a major decision or the confusing signals we get from the people in our lives. We need to make good judgments, ones that account for all the pieces and that pull the pieces together.

I have talked to many people who are trying to figure out how God views a relative who is acting in spiritual rebellion and to many others who are in pain over the eternal destiny of a loved one who recently passed away. Time and again I go back to Genesis 18:25, where Abraham, contemplating the impending judgment of Sodom and Gomorrah, said, "Will not the Judge of all the earth do right?" Abraham was saying, "Surely God makes moral distinctions between good and evil, or else what hope do we have?" When a matter seems too expansive for us to make a judgment, we can trust that God will view it with righteousness and that his response will be just.

LOVE

The Scottish theologian P. T. Forsyth believed there are two overarching attributes of God: holiness and love. Put the pieces together (because God is a whole and complete reality), and you can speak of the holy love of God. His holiness is our assurance that he is different from the defilements of this world and, indeed, different from us, which contradicts any religious notion that God or the gods are just amplified versions of human nature. But because God is love, he is not separated from us. He is engaged, connected, involved. He is a God at work. Separate but not separated. Discriminating but not discriminatory. Hating evil but loving good. And out of that love, he was willing to descend into this corrupt world in a great incarnation and, in the person of Jesus, draw unholy people toward his holiness.

In 1 John 4, we find this clear, bold summary of the issue: "God is love." It is a way of saying that this attribute is so central to who God is, this act is so essential to who we must be in God, that we can set our focus there and spend a lifetime asking God to help us understand and live in that reality. Who will ever tire of adoring a God who is love?

> Dear friends, let us love one another, for love comes from God. Everyone who loves has been born of God and knows God. Whoever does not love does not know God, because God is love. This is how God showed his love among us: He sent his one and only Son into the world that we might live through him. This is love: not that we loved God, but that he loved us and sent his Son as an atoning sacrifice for our sins. Dear friends, since God so loved us, we also ought to love one another. No one has ever seen God; but if we love one another, God lives in us and his love is made complete in us.
>
> —1 JOHN 4:7–12

God's love has many faces. It is his mercy, which is his willingness to suspend judgment while there is hope for correction or salvation in our lives. It is his benevolence, which is his pattern of bringing blessings into our lives. And then, of course, there is grace. Grace is giving. For lack of a better word, it is God's givingness. He gives and gives and gives. No one will ever change that, because love is who God is. And because of love, God does not spoil us. He gives what we really need, which is not always what we think we need.

TRUTH

If God were great but not good, he would manipulate, deceive, and just plain lie. But because he is good, he is true and he is truthful. Saying that God is true is so much more than saying he is accurate (like a bank statement being true or a newspaper report being precise). Truth as a personal attribute means faithfulness. It means being consistent within oneself and in harmony with reality. When any of the biblical authors talked about the "true God," they were saying, "The Creator of heaven and earth is steady and faithful. He does not change the rules of life. All things hold together as they are 'trued' to him who is true." He will always reflect reality to us, and so his words of comfort are not mere sentimental rhetoric, and his words of confrontation are not a sour disposition expressed. There is no one more true than God.

These are all big words—landmark words: Holiness. Righteousness. Justice. Love. Truth. But they are not mere words, and not just theological bookmarkers.

They are themes that rise up out of almost every page of the Bible. They are God's way of saying to you and to me that he is great but he is also good. His moral excellence and purity are who he is. This is why we long for something better in our own lives—to be different from what we are today (more holy), to get things right in life, to receive love and to extend it, to be faithful.

God's majesty alone ought to interest us in knowing him. But it is a good thing if we also pursue him because of his goodness, which is always a picture of how we are to live. That's what it means to be made in the image of God. Some of his attributes, especially the attribute of goodness, are the intended shape of our human lives. And others, like omniscience and omnipresence and omnipotence, are left to God alone.

Here is our hope that the pieces of life can be fit together. Any one of us can look at ourselves and see bits and pieces of rightness, truthfulness, and love. And while these pieces, these shards of broken pottery, are mixed with the decomposing soil of this world and our own nature, they also point to an original wholeness.

I was once on a sandy Mediterranean shore in Israel, at the site of ancient Ashkelon. Now desolate, the place was once an important seaport with great strategic importance. I shuffled around in the sand, looking out at the great sea, and suddenly noticed a pinkish-gray shard of pottery sticking up. As I dug around, I found three or four pieces altogether, which I later confirmed came from biblical times. I couldn't help but wonder, "Where do these pieces come from? What era and what life do they represent?" I could not put the pieces together, and yet their very existence pointed toward a past completeness, a time when they served as part of the everyday life of some Israelite or Phoenician or Philistine family—maybe a pot for oil or a lamp for light.

God is good. And the goodness he has put in this world, though sometimes broken like pottery shards in the sand, keeps pointing us toward the real hope that God will succeed in putting it all together.

PRAY THIS

Dear God, I am glad that you are good. I admit there have been times when I have thought of your immense power but wondered whether your goodness was consistent and whether it touched the real-life situations I see all around me. Help me to see every sign of your goodness that surrounds me. Help me to trust in your goodness when I find myself in bad situations. Please extend your goodness to others through me in some way. Help me to let others know that you created them for goodness and that they can approach you with confidence.

FOR REFLECTION OR DISCUSSION

1. Everyone knows that the word *holiness* is used sparingly today. Why is that? What does the word *holy* connote?
2. What area of your life needs to change?
3. What issue for you right now needs the sober and precise right judgment of God?
4. How have you seen God's love extended to you, and how are you asking him to extend it at this time?
5. Where have you seen or experienced false gods today?

GOD WAS
NEVER ALONE

I am far from pretending to explain
the Trinity so as to render it no longer
a mystery. I think it to be the highest
and deepest of all Divine mysteries still,
notwithstanding anything
that I have said or conceived about it.
I don't intend to explain the Trinity.
—*Jonathan Edwards*

I recently pored over a survey we took in our
church and paused on one of the questions:
"Do you often feel lonely and unnoticed?" A full
75 percent of the respondents said no, which
made me glad for those who had connected with
other people. But my heart went out to the 25
percent who said yes. Loneliness is an awful
place to live. I have had only passing experiences
of loneliness in my life, but each time I have—
usually when far from home and detached from
the people and ordinary fixtures of my life—I
have thought, "May I never be unsympathetic
toward or glib about those who struggle in the
darkened corners of aloneness. I hope I have
eyes to notice the lonely person."

God's great sweeping plan of salvation, his
way of pulling us out of the pit of separation and
self-entrapment and isolation, includes bringing
us into a new community. The blood of Jesus

makes Christians blood brothers and sisters. It is the way of reconciliation and of a humbling leveling. It means finding a new kind of family.

So should it surprise any of us that God himself is a kind of divine communion?

FATHER, SON, AND HOLY SPIRIT

That's what we mean when we speak of God as the Trinity, or in the biblical terms, Father, Son, and Holy Spirit. This was not our idea; it is the way God has shown himself. It is true that the word *Trinity* does not appear in the Bible, but that does not mean that the truth of the Trinity is not there. It was later Christians who tried to think of a single word that summarized this great revelation about the Divine Father, Eternal Son, and Holy Spirit, and so they used *trinitas*, "Trinity," the God who is one and three at the same time.

The first hint came early in Genesis, when God said, "Let *us* make man in *our* image." This was not a chorus of gods like the Greek gods, whom people envisioned living on Mount Olympus in a god-sized melodrama, for the rest of the Old Testament speaks radically of the oneness of God.

Go down any street in Jerusalem today and you will find mounted on Jewish doorposts the heart of the faith of children of Abraham, the *Shema*: "Hear, O Israel: The LORD our God, the LORD is one" (Deut. 6:4). One God, not competing gods. One divine nature, not a clash of supernatural temperaments. One creator over all, not a bevy of regional lords with regional interests and personal idiosyncrasies.

The oneness of God curtails our inclination to keep making new gods—the single voice, the sole object of devotion, the unambiguous source of revelation, the headwaters of spiritual life. God's oneness is his strength, his purity, and his simplicity. His oneness is our assurance that there is not a competing Dark Lord who pulls toward evil as hard as God pulls toward good, while we wait breathlessly, hoping that the good will win out in the end.

ALTERNATIVE VIEWS OF GOD

Before going further with the Christian understanding of God, we should note the main alternative views of who or what God is.

Atheism, or *materialism*, is the view that there is no God. As a dogma or philosophy, atheism says that there is a physical universe and nothing else. Belief in God is a weak-minded explanation or naive wishful thinking that prevents people from standing on their own two feet.

Polytheism is the belief that there are many gods. The polytheist says, "In our tribe we worship this god, but you live on the other side of the river (or across the ocean, or in a different culture), and you worship a different god. We choose to accept a plurality of gods because we're not about to believe in your god, and we don't care a bit if you believe in our god." There is no absolute God to whom you are fully accountable. Less-than-almighty gods tend not to make absolute demands.

Pantheism holds that there is a divine nature in the universe, but it is indistinguishable from the physical universe itself. God is not separate; God is what is. God is "it," not "he" or "she." God may be not even an "it" but rather a divine quality that pervades the cosmos. Pantheism deifies the earth and the self. It holds that if we have within us an urge to find the divine, it is because *we* are divine and part of a spiritual unity that binds together all reality. Pantheism says that your search for God doesn't need to stretch any further than what you can see. What it does not offer is a God who is better than us, higher than us, stronger than us.

Deism is the belief that God created the universe, but then he stepped back from it all and has no controlling influence over or involvement in the world. There are no miracles—never have been. There is no word from heaven—never has been. Don't expect any direct divine involvement in your life—never will be. The Bible is a human book with spiritual aspirations, but ignore the miracles (including the resurrection of Jesus), because we know better than that today.

That brings us to *theism*, the historic Christian view. A confidence that when you pray, there is a God who hears you. An anticipation about what new movement God is going to initiate in the world today. An attentiveness to the voice of God. A confidence in divine love. A belief that God acts with intelligent purpose. Theism is the belief that there is a God who is singular, transcendent, all-powerful, consistent, and wise. And he is personal.

God Is Personal

What is a person? You are a person; a stone isn't. You have self-aware-ness; a tree doesn't. You can be moral; electricity can't. You are alive; a corpse is not. *Person* usually refers to a living human being, although from a Christian point of view it also refers to God, and we assume that we are persons with personalities because a personal God created us.

One day when I was in college, I drove through a housing project in Chicago in my black and orange, German-made Opel, engaged in a discussion with a clergyman on the issue of what makes human beings distinct. What do we mean when we say we have (or are) liv-ing souls? This young, well-educated minister, who sincerely believed that the way to spiritual freedom is to give up any infantile notion of the metaphysical, to stop believing that we are any more than well-adapted animals, pointed to a stone on the street where we parked and said, "I believe that stone has as much soul as I do." A stone. I was stunned. I was crestfallen. I was still piecing together my faith, and here was a man who saw our personhood, derived from God, as no more than a hunk of earth.

Some people do acknowledge that God is absolute, mighty, and rational but believe God is more a supernatural force than a divine person. But the God of the Bible is a person. He is intelligent, cre-ative, and moral. He speaks of himself as "I." Indeed, the idea that God speaks at all assumes that he is a personal being. God plans; God acts; God intends. He has will and wisdom. He has many names. He wants us to know him. If God were not personal, we could not pray, and we would not worship. If God were merely a force, we would have no guidance, no comfort, no discipline.

One of the defining characteristics of a person is the ability to engage in relationships. Stones don't have relationships. Persons talk to each other, they seek to understand each other, they make choices that shape their relationships with each other. Persons (from *persona*, "mask") have faces, or public presentations of themselves. Unlike stars or water or trees, persons interact dynamically with each other. Persons know other persons—not just know about or store information on but comprehend, care for, and commit to.

I have to admit that when our children were born, I probably didn't really see them as persons. They appeared to be little creatures we served by putting food in one end and cleaning up the by-products from the other. My wife, of course, saw this as a wonderful relationship, but I was really waiting for the first ball game or the first swim in the lake. But it didn't take that long for me to connect more deeply. All it took was for that first responsive smile to spread across that small face—eyes wide open, a gutteral "g-aaaaa," which meant something or other. See a smile and you think, "There's a person in there! And I want to know what's behind the smile."

THE GOD OF ABRAHAM, ISAAC, AND JACOB

After Blaise Pascal, the famous French mathematician and philosopher, died in 1662, a piece of paper was found in the lining of his coat. So important to him were the words written on this paper (which he had written eight years earlier) that he kept them close to his body day after day. The scrap, which contained his central convictions, read: *Dieu d'Abraham, Dieu d'Isaac, Dieu de Jacob, non des philosophes et savants.* (God of Abraham, God of Isaac, God of Jacob, not of the philosophers and the learned.) These words followed: *Certitude. Certitude. Sentiment. Joie. Paix.* (Certainty. Certainty. Feeling. Joy. Peace.) According to the calculations of this mathematician and vivid believer, among the multitude of competing deities, there is one who is a real, live God, who moved in history and who introduced himself by name to people like Abraham, Isaac, and Jacob. And if he was known by them, he could be known by Blaise—and by anybody named Juan, Jessica, Michael, Kwame, and by you and me.

Pascal, however, did not invent the appellation "God of Abraham, God of Isaac, God of Jacob." It was first heard by Moses, when he stood before a mysterious bush that was on fire but was not consumed. He heard his name being called, "Moses! Moses!" and then he heard a name for God, a grand introduction at a watershed moment in history: "I am . . . the God of Abraham, the God of Isaac, and the God of Jacob," and Moses hid his face (Ex. 3:6).

Though God does not have a physical face, he does dynamically interact with us, as when, in the desert of Sinai, he introduced himself as "the God of Abraham, the God of Isaac, and the God of Jacob." This is no ethereal description of a divine force, no abstract set of metaphysical (beyond the physical) characteristics. God was saying to Moses, "I am the one who came to people such as Abraham, called them, motivated them, instructed them, inspired them, protected them, fed them, and corrected them. I am the one who made promises and entered into covenants, who had compassion when they suffered, and who stood with them against evildoers. I am a personal God, which is why you can speak with me and listen to me. Most important, you can trust me." Had God not said that, perhaps Moses would have thought of him as "the god of mysterious fire," or "the god of desert magic," or "Baal-bush."

God is the "I AM," and he would soon tell Moses to tell the people that "I AM" had sent him. Imagine the world if human beings stopped thinking of God as an "it" that they are trying to discover like some new astrophysical phenomenon and realized that "I AM" is searching us out.

What Moses didn't know is that this introduction was the prelude to a whole new phase of divine activity in the world. God was about to move, and Moses would be his chosen servant. This Person-God was about to snatch a people out of bitter slavery. He was about to bring them to a mountain representing his unchanging nature and there offer thousands of words of law and grace, ceremony and celebration, truth and order. Moses, the meekest man on earth, as he was called, was about to be swept up in a great divine saving movement.

If you are inclined to ask yourself, "What kind of God do I believe in?" then don't think you're just deciding which "-ism" you hold to. The question is, If you were to write your central conviction on a scrap of paper and sew it into your everyday garment, close to your heart, what would you write?

Here is something worth wearing close to your heart: "I believe in a God who is above all and with all, powerful beyond all measure and personal beyond all imagining. I believe in a God whom I can talk to and a God who speaks to me. I believe in the God of Abraham, Isaac, and Jacob. And I believe in this same God who became a face, a true face, when he came in the person of Jesus Christ."

The Creator is one, but the One said, "Let *us* make man in *our* image," and in that revelatory moment we learn that we are like God and that we are very unlike God. "Like" because we are created in his image. Of the many things *image* and *likeness* might mean—that we are creative because God is creative, spiritual because God is Spirit, intelligent because God is rational—"in his image" may also mean that we are communal creatures because we were created by a communal God. In other words, because of the divine communion of the Trinity, we were created with the ability and the longing to be friends, brothers, sisters, aunts, grandfathers, coworkers, teammates, spouses, colleagues, and neighbors. We are in pain when we are lonely. We long to connect. Adam needs a companion.

"In Our Image"

Because God is Father, Son, and Holy Spirit, it had to be "our," not "my." And here, too, is part of that image. "In the image of God he created him, male and female he created them." Many Bible interpreters believe that the diversity of maleness and femaleness is as central to that image as anything else. God created not just a him, but also a her—a them. Unlike the philosophies and religions that portray the ideal as the blurring together of all things into a divine oneness, the Scriptures teach that the essential created nature of all things—the "image" of God in man—displays the splendor of diversity with unity.

Image bearers will therefore authenticate and enhance the natural variations in the human family. In the church, that means celebrating one body, many members. We will not criticize, demean, devalue, or ignore other brothers or sisters just because they are different. We will not just grudgingly go along with the principle of unity. We will long for unity, love unity. As with our physical bodies, we will feel most healthy when we are whole. God's image makes us a "them." And so we will relinquish the idea of the self-reliant individual. We just weren't meant to play tennis solo.

Image bearers keep seeking God because they are distinctly spiritual creatures. Prayer is as necessary as breathing. Worship is that valued time of showing respect for God and scrambling under the protective wings of his lordship, as chicks gather under a hen's wings.

Image bearers strive to understand and follow the "oughtness" of life's plan. They will celebrate morality. They will not be embarrassed that they cannot participate in activities that the masses may seek. They will not feel left out or that they are missing out. They will accept the added responsibility that comes with added knowledge.

Image bearers will not make their life's aim the crafting and polishing of their own image but will realize that our only hope is if God remakes our image again, that image so broken and tarnished by sin and evil in the world and in us.

EXPLAINING THE TRINITY

But we also realize we are unlike God in that none of us are one and three in ourselves—at least not like God is. Some have thought that maybe we have three aspects that are analogous to the Trinity (body, soul, spirit, for instance), but none of us will be like Father, Son, and Holy Spirit. God's oneness and threeness is unique to God.

Many people reject the idea of the Trinity out of hand as a violation of mathematical law. One does not equal three on any calculator, so there can't be a triune God. But divine reality is not subsumed under simple arithmetic. A God who creates all and who is worth worshiping will stretch beyond all our normal perceptions of the way physical things and beings work. God dwells in dimensions we cannot even imagine.

For centuries, some Christians have tried to explain the Trinity with analogies of the physical world, with good motive but with limited results. I've heard children taught in Sunday school that the Trinity is like water, which can exist in three forms—ice, liquid, and steam. Or like an egg, which has shell, white, and yolk. Early Christians used far better analogies, like source, spring, and stream; sun, ray, and light; or root, shoot, and fruit. But here's the limitation: comparing the God of glory and might to any physical reality is a far-distant comparison and tells us little about what the living God is really like. God is simply not like water any more than Susan, a human being, is like, say, a coconut.

Others have used analogies from human personality, which is perhaps a bit closer to the mark. Augustine said that as a human being is one creature with distinct inner senses—such as memory, understanding, and will—so the Trinity is one and three. The problem with that analogy is that Father, Son, and Spirit truly interact with each other and speak of each other, which is not true of the different aspects of our psyches.

Some early Christian thinkers said the Trinity is like Peter, James, and John—three personalities but one shared humanity. The problem here, of course, is that three men are three beings, but God is one being. The Bible nowhere allows us to think there are three Gods. Nor will it do to go to the opposite extreme and think of God as an actor who changes costumes with each successive part of a three-act play (an idea known as modalism, for the successive modes God uses to manifest himself to us).

At one time, at all times, and for eternity, there is Father, Son, and Holy Spirit, the utterly unique divine communion. Together they crafted the universe in the beginning, appeared in and spoke to and shaped the history of Israel, and lovingly interacted in the great plan of redeeming broken, lonely human lives.

At the baptism of Jesus, the Spirit descended like a dove, and the Father spoke words like thunder without lightning that authenticated the Son. "This is my Son, whom I love; with him I am well pleased." Three of Jesus' disciples—Peter, James, and John—also heard the Father's voice from heaven on the day Jesus was bathed in the light of glory on the Mount of Transfiguration. The voice from heaven repeated the same words as at the baptism, "This is my Son, whom I love; with him I am well pleased," with the added statement "Listen to him!" The Father was proclaiming that the work of the Son was the work of the Father. One God, one work, Father and Son saving the world with the Spirit.

Jesus spoke of his relation to the Father—about being sent, and being obedient, and being one. Jesus went out to begin his mission in the power of the Spirit, who would be sent too. All of this tells us that the Trinity is dynamically engaged in the matters of this world with varied roles at different times, but no member of the Trinity is less divine than the other because of the roles. Between Creator and created is a bold and unambiguous line. Father, Son, and Spirit are on one side of the line, and everything else—absolutely everything else—is on the other.

We get a glimpse behind the veil of cosmic history in John's words: "In the beginning was the Word, and the Word was with God, and the Word was God." How could we possibly grasp more than that? Of course, we will go on asking questions as long as we have spiritual curiosity. Jesus spoke about the Holy Spirit (especially in John 14–16) and about the Father's relation with the Spirit. And Jesus' last command, the marching orders for his followers forever, was to baptize people "in the name of the Father and of the Son and of the Holy Spirit" (Matt. 28:19). One name but three names. This is the mark every believing Christian bears from his or her baptism on. What a mark it is!

The apostles used Trinitarian phrases as theological landmarks pointing us again and again to the divine communion. One example is the benediction at the end of 2 Corinthians: "May the grace of the Lord Jesus Christ, and the love of God, and the fellowship of the Holy Spirit be with you all." Like Jesus' last command, these are words chosen carefully to echo in our spirits, to lock us into the basic structure of all reality. In this world of shifting and cracking and crumbling foundations, here are three anchor points, three benefactors touching our lives in so many ways. Provider and protector because he is Father; teacher, friend, and sacrifice because he is Christ; mighty force, living wind, and filling inspiration because he is Holy Spirit.

Whenever we feel that life is too complicated or too fractured—too many pieces to sort out, too much diversity, too many differences—then the Trinity, the God who is one and who is three, reminds us that he built unity and diversity into the very design of life. We can trust in the unity, and we should relish the diversity. That is our one hope of getting along with each other in our communities. He is a God of peace, not a God in pieces.

Here is a God we can worship and adore at every possible level. Prayer is drawn out of us by the irresistible pull to speak with Abba, Rabbi, and Spirit. Because of the Trinity, we know there is always a God to talk to, a God to know. When we think of prayer from a Trinitarian point of view, we see prayer not as a mechanical duty but as a lively exchange with a God of personality, action, and fullness.

This is how we are to understand the natural world in which we live. Could God have created a world with just a handful of species instead of thousands? Of course he could have, but the Trinity was not inclined to make things that crudely. Could God have avoided racial warfare by creating a single race? Or could he have kept things simpler by creating one gender instead of two? Yes, but that would not have been good enough for the Trinity. Every racist, every misogynist, and every child-abuser chooses to live by the principle of one kind of human being dominating another. But this is an utter violation of God's creation. God ordained that his creation would be a community, which requires human beings to treat each other with enormous respect. Creation note after creation note created a true symphony. You need pieces to make an orchestra. But when the conductor puts the pieces together, the sound that comes out is richer than the best soloist could ever achieve. It takes more effort to put pieces together, but do we have anything better to do with our time and energy?

Another dramatic outcome of a faith in a triune God: the spiritual community that the divine communion creates and shapes. Who else but a triune God would work people together and bind them together in the way that he does? The verses in 1 Corinthians 12:4–6 put it best: "There are different kinds of gifts, but the same Spirit. There are different kinds of service, but the same Lord. There are different kinds of working, but the same God works all of them in all men." It is because of the Trinity, in other words, that I am bound together with Bill, and Susan, and Craig, and with all the ushers, musicians, evangelists, custodians, missionaries, fifth graders, eleventh graders, and the seventy-something brothers and sisters in Christ's church. It is because of the Trinity that others are present when I am discouraged or disobedient or lonely. The Trinity is the reason I can hope for a good marriage or to love as a good father. The Trinity connects me to generations past and to human beings not yet conceived, but in the mind of God.

The Trinity is not a problem to solve but a reality to grasp (as much as we can) with wonder and awe. Would you want a God, worship a God, or serve a God who was simple to understand and who followed our rules of arithmetic? Isn't it awe-inspiring to discover that God is the singular Lord and Master over all but also is alive within himself, in a communion that has always and will always exist with a unified purpose and love?

There is no better assurance that we are not alone now and never will be alone. Why?

Because God was never alone.

Before a single speck of matter existed and long before angels, cedars, rhinos, and the man and the woman were created, God was alive in a communion of love and concord.

> Praise God from whom all blessings flow.
> Praise him all creatures here below.
> Praise him above ye heavenly host.
> Praise Father, Son, and Holy Ghost.

PRAY THIS

I believe, heavenly Father, that you are the source and strength of all good things. I believe, Lord Jesus, that you are my best master because you were with the Father before time began and will reign with him on one throne for all time to come. I believe, Holy Spirit, that right now, today, you are exerting your mighty power all over the world in the continuing mission to save us from ourselves. Holy, holy, holy are you, Lord God, Almighty.

FOR REFLECTION OR DISCUSSION

1. What one thought about the Trinity do you have right now that you would like to ponder further?
2. Has belief in the Trinity been a problem, a joy, or an irrelevancy for you?
3. What new steps in prayer do you think you could take by focusing on the Trinity?
4. How would things be different if Jesus were merely the best human prophet in history?
5. Which of the Scripture passages quoted in this chapter would you like to reflect on further?

PUTTING
ON FLESH

11

If God had a name what would it be?
And would you call it to his face?
If you were faced with him in all his glory
What would you ask if you had just one
   question? . . .
What if God was one of us?
—*Joan Osborne, "One of Us"*

He shouldn't have gone out in the ice storm on that cold day in 1841, not even for his inauguration as president of the United States, and certainly not without a hat or coat. And he shouldn't have given a ponderous 8,495-word inaugural address that took almost two hours to deliver. But that's what sixty-eight-year-old Henry Harrison did. He developed pneumonia and died a month later, holding the shortest presidential term in history. He accomplished nothing of what he had aspired to in his address.

I have often wondered what it must be like to be inaugurated into some high office, say, that of prime minister or president, and to know you have a limited amount of time in which to accomplish something of significance. The inauguration of a president in the United States, for instance, is an opportunity for a whole nation, and for other nations of interest, to take an accounting of all the problems that need to be fixed and all the new initiatives that need to be taken. Some pieces put back together and other pieces put together for the very first time. How would you prevent being overwhelmed by all that needed attention? Wouldn't high-minded words of lofty aspirations seem like so much wishful thinking? Within days, reality would hit, and the push and pull of all the human contests and conflicts would take over.

Maybe that's why some inaugurations have been extraordinarily simple, such as Thomas Jefferson's talk before a few close friends before he retired to Conrad's Tavern to eat his dinner alone. Or the party at the White House on Andrew Jackson's big day, with common folks breaking crystal, muddying the carpets, and spitting tobacco juice on the floor. (The hosts did regain control by moving tubs of liquor to the back lawn after Jackson had escaped by jumping out a back window.) By contrast, the presidential inauguration in 2000 included sixty-two balls and a $40 million price tag.

George Washington's first inaugural address focused simply on two things: his inadequacies for the tasks of the presidential office, and the importance of acknowledging the providence of God and the necessity of God's guidance for the future. And his second inaugural address was just 135 words long and took two minutes to deliver.

One has to be careful what one promises to accomplish.

If *christos*, meaning "Anointed One" (*messhiach*, "Messiah," in Hebrew), is an office of sorts, what was Jesus claiming to accomplish when he let people conclude that he was the Anointed One?

The human race knew the Anointed One was coming. He simply had to come, being the kind of God that he is. He is good and he is great. He must have heard our cries for help. He must have an escape route for us, some healing power for our misery.

To hear that "God became flesh" is at once one of the most shocking claims you will ever hear and one of the most obvious. We knew he was coming because he is a saving kind of God.

So, long before Christ did come, people imagined in their storytelling a day when God, or one of the gods, might come to earth. He might even suffer and die. And certainly he would rise up from death. The existence of numerous such stories or myths does not take anything away from Jesus' incarnation; they emphasize it. That a Savior would come to earth is a truth so obvious that it echoes throughout history—across civilizations and deep in the heart even of those who have never heard the proclamation that God has come. Now and again, even today someone will discover a primitive tribe which expects that some kind of divine Savior will come.

WHY GOD BECAME MAN

He had to come. We knew he would.

In the eleventh century, a wise Christian by the name of Anselm wrote a small book called *Cur Deus Homo* (*Why God Became Man*), in which he offered a straightforward interpretation of salvation. Anselm said that only man *should* solve the problem of sin, but only God *could*. Who ought to suffer the consequences for the mistakes and crimes of human beings? Human beings, of course. But the problem is we cannot really pay for our own sins. We were designed as creatures of perfect goodness and nobility. So every failing, every negligence, every assault against another person puts us deeper and deeper into a moral deficit. No one can make up for all that.

No one, that is, except God.

Only man *should* solve the problem of sin, but only God *could*. And so God became man. Now, Christians don't believe this because it is a neat, logical solution. We believe it because of the whole eye-opening, mind-blowing, assumption-shattering experience we have had with Jesus Christ since he came. Jesus' claims about why he came have proven true many times over, in the lives of countless human beings from almost every culture in the world.

The beloved disciple, John, explained it this way: "In the beginning was the Word, and the Word was with God, and the Word was God. . . . The Word became flesh and made his dwelling among us. We have seen his glory, the glory of the One and Only, who came from the Father, full of grace and truth" (John 1:1, 14). John talked about the truth that most gripped his life, a reality that bonded him to men and women with whom he would otherwise have nothing in common: "That which was from the beginning, which we have heard, which we have seen with our eyes, which we have looked at and our hands have touched—this we proclaim concerning the Word of life. The life appeared ... to us.... We write this to make our joy complete" (1 John 1:1–2, 4). John also said, "Every spirit that acknowledges that Jesus Christ has come in the flesh is from God, but every spirit that does not acknowledge Jesus is not from God" (1 John 4:2–3).

The incarnation was not a divine visitation in the mere form of a human being. Jesus was no holograph of divinity. Some ancient self-described sophisticates, called Gnostics, wanted to make Christianity more spiritual than it already was and said that the Savior only appeared to be human and to possess real flesh. He was a superspiritual being who came to impart cryptic saving knowledge. If you could understand this coded truth and grasp the lingo, you would be enlightened, and thus saved by the knowledge. They even said that the Savior went nowhere near the cross. He switched identities with Simon of Cyrene, the man who was forced to carry Jesus' cross, and then stood at a distance, laughing at the foolish Romans who thought they had nailed to the cross the man who claimed to be the Messiah.

But the Gnostics, of ancient days and of today, are wrong. The Messiah didn't laugh on that day because he had fooled people into thinking he was a human being, while he skirted around the torture of the cross. Rather, he took the pain of the world on himself and in that abject agony offered the way out for us. As wrong and unjust and inexcusable as it was, the death of Jesus also makes perfect sense. It all fits into the consistent pattern of God's character, the nature of the corrupt world, and the love that God has for those he created in his own image. All the pieces fit. The mission to put the world back together was itself coming together. God was doing what only God could do.

There are many others who say Jesus lived as a man but deny any possibility that he was divine. This should not surprise us. The incarnation is a truth that exceeds our comprehension. It breaks the rules of the way we think things always are. Try explaining to a five-year-old that the sun, which we all know so well, is one star among millions in our galaxy, and that our galaxy, like a small cloud in the blackness, is only one among millions of other galaxies, and that it all stretches out for billions of light-years, and you'll see the line of comprehension crossed quite quickly. So I, for one, am not at all surprised that the truth that divinity became flesh, the Word became Jesus, the Son became the son of a carpenter, exceeds the processing power of the little computer inside my skull, which can't even comprehend the properties of a sole atom.

No one who believes in the incarnation should suppose that we can get into Jesus' head and understand his coexisting divinity and humanity. We can barely understand our own inner lives. No special psychology text has ever been written about it, and there never will be.

Who Christ Is

Now this is what Christians since the earliest days have said about the person of Christ: He is clearly one person, not some dualistic oddity. But in that one person are definitely two full and distinct natures. Jesus was truly human, not just a human form in which divinity replaced human nature. And he was truly divine, not just a prophet, nor even a superprophet, who was invested with an extraordinary measure of divine power.

How do we know this? First, we know Jesus was truly divine because he demonstrated the unique *attributes of deity*. Power when wind and waves obeyed him and when he took a dead little girl by the hand and she woke up. Holiness, glory, and omniscience. "Come, see a man who told me everything I ever did. Could this be the Christ?" (John 4:29).

Second, we know Jesus was truly divine because he exercised the *prerogatives of deity*. He wielded authority by calling himself "the Lord of the Sabbath" and by saying astounding things such as "Heaven and earth will pass away, but my words will never pass away." He forgave people their sins. Who but God can do that? Which is why, when Jesus told a paralytic man that he forgave his sins, Jesus' opponents snarled, "Why does this fellow talk like that? He's blaspheming! Who can forgive sins but God alone?" They had no idea how right they were. Jesus also said that he would be involved in judgment: "When the Son of Man comes in his glory . . . he will separate the people one from another as a shepherd separates the sheep from the goats." He solicited faith in himself: "I am the way and the truth and the life. No one comes to the Father except through me." And most remarkable of all, he let other people worship him: the disciples in the boat after he calmed the storm, Mary in the garden after the resurrection, even the magi, who came to worship him as a baby in Bethlehem.

What does worship mean in these contexts? In the boat, Jesus' disciples had no hymnals, no guitars, no offering plates. What they did have was themselves and the ability to bow down or bend the knee in the presence of the one they recognized as Lord supreme. They were compelled to do it. Bowing was as quick a response as when you squint or put your hand up when you step from a dark room out into the blazing sun. Later they must have pondered the significance of their impulse to worship the man they were following.

Third, we know Jesus was truly divine because the statements he made amounted to *claims of deity*. "I and the Father are one." "Anyone who has seen me has seen the Father." "All that belongs to the Father is mine." His opponents began considering murder because "not only was he breaking the Sabbath, but he was even calling God his own Father, making himself equal with God."

And fourth, we know Jesus was truly divine because he referred to himself, as did those around him, with *names of deity*. Jesus said, "Before Abraham was born, I am!" (which recalls the special name God used with Moses, "I AM WHO I AM"). Thomas fell at Jesus' feet after he knew Jesus had risen from the dead, exclaiming, "My Lord and my God!" When people called Jesus "Lord," it seemed to go well beyond the meaning of "master." Jesus also referred to himself as "Son of God" and "Son of Man," labels that expectant Jews knew identified the coming Messiah.

So during the brief earthly ministry of Jesus, his disciples accumulated a picture of who Jesus of Nazareth really was. Plenty of evidence pointed to the fact that he was not just from Nazareth. He came from God's place, with a divine mission, and the picture of Jesus was getting more astounding all the time. Jesus' disciples strained to add up all the pieces of evidence in the immediacy of the events. Like a giant puzzle, the pieces came together, but it would take time for people to step back far enough from the puzzle to see the picture the pieces made.

What is the sum of it all? C. S. Lewis put it this way in *Mere Christianity*: "I am trying here to prevent anyone saying the really foolish thing that people often say about Him: 'I'm ready to accept Jesus as a great moral teacher, but I don't accept His claim to be God.' A man who was merely a man and said the sort of things Jesus said would not be a great moral teacher. He would either be a lunatic—on a level with a man who says he is a poached egg—or else he would be the Devil of Hell. You must make your choice. Either this man was, and is, the Son of God; or else a madman or something worse."

What was Jesus trying to accomplish? The answer to that question is bound up in the person Jesus is. He was able to do what he did because of the person he is. He made an exodus for people, a way out of entanglements with self, the heavy gravity of sin, and the assassination plots of the Evil One.

And Jesus didn't just try to pull it off. It all worked. He was there at the beginning when God said, "Let us make a universe," and then rested. He was there on the cross when he committed his spirit to his Father, but only after saying, "It is finished." And the "it" was an agenda that, from his inauguration, the beginning of his earthly ministry, he was uniquely capable of fulfilling: the salvation of the shattered human race.

PRAY THIS

Lord Jesus, you said you will bless those who do not see you and yet still believe. So I count myself blessed. I am grateful that I can read your teachings and hear the testimony of those who saw your miraculous acts. Teach me to know you as the living Word, and help me to understand the full meaning of the fact that you came and took on human nature. Thank you for doing that out of your love for those you created.

FOR REFLECTION OR DISCUSSION

1. What did you believe as a child about Jesus, and how has that changed over the years?
2. What aspects of "God became flesh" seem mysterious to you?
3. How would salvation be different if Jesus were just a moral teacher?
4. What would you have thought if you had been there to see what Jesus did and to hear what he said? How would you respond if you witnessed something like that today?

RESCUE

12

> I think nothing has surprised us more
> than to learn so many ships were near
> enough to rescue us in a few hours.
> —Titanic *survivor*

Surely she would escape from her kidnappers if she had the slightest chance, everyone assumed. If she had any opportunity to call out to someone for help or to pass a note that said, "I'm Elizabeth Smart. Help me," she would. And so, for the nine months of her captivity, since she had been snatched from her bedroom in the middle of the night, most people assumed the worst: she must be dead.

Yet fourteen-year-old Elizabeth was very much alive. During her captivity she had been around many people yet had not signaled for help. She was left alone at times and could have walked away. When police approached her on the street, inquiring whether she was Elizabeth Smart, she denied it. This poor young girl, practically brainwashed by her domineering abductors, needed so much to be saved but didn't see it and couldn't take advantage of opportunities to escape. It was a good thing the police officer who recognized her on the street knew better and was determined to find the truth.

Then there is the case of Jessica Lynch, the nineteen-year-old private first class who served as part of a maintenance unit in Iraq and was taken captive after her convoy took a wrong turn in the city of Nasiriyah. Held for eight days in an Iraqi hospital, she cried out to go home. But she could not save herself. Even if there are no armed guards, how do you run when you have two broken legs? A few days later rescuers swooped down by helicopter, stormed the building, snatched her from her bed, and carried her to safety.

SAVED FROM WHAT?

Today some people think it's a joke when they hear, "You must be saved." "That's the kind of thing religious kooks say," they think. "Isn't salvation an antique idea, or maybe just the mental crutch of some people who still aren't willing to stand on their own two feet, spiritually speaking? Isn't it just derelicts who need to 'come to Jesus'?"

But what if you have two broken legs? What if you have no idea just how much trouble you are in and how desperately you need to be saved?

Almost all religions begin with the assumption that we need to be saved from that something that is dreadfully wrong in the world—or with us. Salvation is a belief and a hope that there is a way out of captivity, a rescue, whether or not we know we need it.

Christian faith says specifically that we need to be saved from evil, from judgment, and from our own self-destructive sin. Salvation from evil means that God will prevent the human race from descending into the deepest darkness, even though evil will keep on appearing in tomorrow's headlines until God comes to remake the world. Salvation from judgment means that, by God's gracious act of free forgiveness, he acquits us of the spiritual crimes and misdemeanors we have committed. And salvation from sin means that God's power is available to reshape our character so that we need not repeat the same mistakes over and over.

That is precisely why the Bible speaks of salvation as a past, present, and future reality. The biblical authors say we have been saved, we are being saved, and we will be saved.

Looking to the past, the truth is that "it is by grace you have been saved, through faith—and this is not from yourselves, it is the gift of God—not by works, so that no one can boast" (Eph. 2:8–9).

"You have been saved." God has already won the war, though the battles continue. He has sent his grace, his unstoppable intent to pour out mercy and kindness, to the human race like food for the starving and water for the parched. When Jesus died on the cross, the clash between the political powers of earth, the dark power of the demonic, and the brilliant power of God came to a decisive climax. The light went out for three hours; the body of the author of life slumped against the rough wood. Perhaps Satan laughed, and then cowered. The curtain in the temple was torn open as a sign, as if this High Priest had stepped up to the Holy of Holies, the presence of God, and ripped open an entryway that would forever make a relationship with God only as far away as the words "I believe. I do believe."

But God is also continuing to save us. The battles still rage on, though the outcome is certain. Writing from prison, the apostle Paul said, "Continue to *work out your salvation* with fear and trembling," and then, to make sure that people with broken legs didn't try to run too soon, he added, "for it is God who works in you to will and to act according to his good purpose" (Phil. 2:12–13, italics mine). He also wrote, "The message of the cross is foolishness to those who are perishing, but to us who *are being saved* it is the power of God" (1 Cor. 1:18, italics mine). The process of salvation is God's faithful, constant work of educating us and shaping us and cleansing us: "I will save you from all your uncleanness" (Ezek. 36:29). That means that the wisest person is the one who says, "I am unclean, I can't get the dirt off, I can't heal myself. God, please do what only you can."

Then there is future salvation. God *will* save us. Stop for just for a moment to ask yourself what you really believe is going to happen as history unfolds in ever-greater extremes.

Charles Dickens's famous opening passage in *A Tale of Two Cities* begins this way: "It was the best of times, it was the worst of times, it was the age of wisdom, it was the age of foolishness, it was the epoch of belief, it was the epoch of incredulity, it was the season of light, it was the season of darkness, it was the spring of hope, it was the winter of despair, we had everything before us, we had nothing before us, we were all going direct to Heaven, we were all going direct the other way."

Doesn't the world today look like just such a set of contradictions? But today it's even more severe. The pendulum is swinging in an ever-wider arch: the best is getting better, and the worst is getting worse. History still moves toward a clash. The question of destiny should press itself on every person's mind. Some take comfort in the roll of the dice, thinking the chances are good that they will be able to duck the clash. But whether any of us witness firsthand the climax of history, we will all face the last doorway when we come to the end of our own lives. We all need the God who says, "In the day of salvation I will help you" (Isa. 49:8). We all need to heed the advice that "the hour has come for you to wake up from your slumber, because our salvation is nearer now than when we first believed" (Rom. 13:11).

The biblical word *salvation* means "rescue." It means that someone bigger and better, stronger and wiser, does for us what we cannot do for ourselves. The necessity of salvation takes nothing away from human dignity. Rather, it gives us back our own lives. Whether or not we realize we need to be rescued, we still need to be rescued. It just makes sense for us to admit it and to live in such a way that we respond to the rescue.

Two thousand years ago, a young woman named Mary had the wisdom to know she needed God's salvation. She wasn't a captive to any abductor, but she knew she was trapped by her own limitations and as vulnerable as anyone else to a wicked neighbor, a political regime, or physical injury. Her song celebrated God's mighty ways of rescuing us: "My soul glorifies the Lord and my spirit rejoices in God my Savior. . . . His mercy extends to those who fear him, from generation to generation. He has performed mighty deeds with his arm" (Luke 1:46, 50–51).

Mary's song was her response to the most incredible claim, given to her by an angel: "You will be with child and give birth to a son, and you are to give him the name Jesus."

Jesus in English, *Yeshua* in Hebrew, is a name that simply means "salvation." As Joseph heard from an angel in a dream, "She will give birth to a son, and you are to give him the name Jesus, because he will save his people from their sins."

Salvation has two sides: the objective and the subjective. The first is the fact of salvation. By Jesus' coming and by his sacrificial death and resurrection to new life, an unalterable act of salvation has occurred. The Bible has a whole vocabulary to explain it: redemption, reconciliation, justification, adoption.

Redemption, a word from the world of the marketplace, says that through the sacrificial death of Christ, we have been bought out of our slavery to sin. Like one who purchases slaves only to set them free, God supplied the price and received the price. All of this was depicted again and again in the sacrificial rituals of the Old Testament. We are truly free, but our freedom comes from being owned by God: "You are not your own; you were bought at a price. Therefore honor God with your body" (1 Cor. 6:19–20).

Reconciliation comes from the world of relationships. The shattering effects of sin in the world led to estrangement. We are separated from each other and separated from God. But in Christ, and in his sacrifice, God provides a bridge. Through faith, we are on God's side and God calls us his friends.

Adoption, from the realm of the family, means that we become, through the sacrifice of Christ, true children of God. All human beings are creations of God and are thus his offspring. But being a true child of God is a reality of a different magnitude. It means being an heir and living in conscious submission to the master of the household, the benevolent Father. The prodigal son became a son again when he turned back toward home.

Justification is from the world of law courts. *Justification* and *righteousness* are in the same word group in the New Testament. To be justified means to be made right with God. It is what happened to Abraham when he believed God's astounding promise. Justification by grace through faith is a foundation of certainty. As Paul put it: "If God is for us, who can be against us? He who did not spare his own Son, but gave him up for us all—how will he not also, along with him, graciously give us all things? Who will bring any charge against those whom God has chosen? It is God who justifies. Who is he that condemns?" (Rom. 8:31–34).

So the New Testament makes it clear in a multitude of ways that we need to be rescued and that the rescue is real. It isn't just about getting snatched away from someone who has kidnapped you; it is about a lifetime of being joined to the family of God and to God himself.

But we must believe we need to be rescued. We need to let God pull us away from our captivity so that the confusion in our minds can clear up. And then *saved* will be one of the most precious words in our vocabulary.

PRAY THIS

> *Lord, I know that sometimes I try to tell myself that I really don't need to be rescued. And I realize how foolish that is. It is easier for me to ignore my real spiritual needs than to face them. But in your saving arms are kindness, grace, and mercy. You have done for me what I cannot do for myself. So please help me loosen my grip on my own life and experience your daily saving work in my life.*

FOR REFLECTION OR DISCUSSION

1. Can you think of a time in your life when you were in trouble and didn't fully realize it?
2. What are the kinds of things that people need to be freed from?
3. What are some stereotypical views of salvation that might be misleading or prove unhelpful?
4. How would you seek God's rescue in your life at this time?

CROSS AND TOMB

13

> He who knows the mystery
> of the cross and tomb, also knows the
> essential principles of all things.
> — *Maximus Confessor*

I was walking through the tiled corridor of the history building at the University of Wisconsin, having just finished teaching a class, my mind focused on pressing ahead to the cafeteria for a bite to eat. But my way was blocked by a cluster of twenty or so students who stood motionless and quiet, staring up at a TV monitor in the lobby, listening to the news anchor's low and slow voice, which echoed among the tile and stone. I too could only stop and look up.

There on the monitor was a picture of a few dozen people in an outdoor reviewing stand, and they too were looking up, straining to see something, heads tilting, hands shielding their eyes from the sun. The next shot was of a strange pillar of smoke that branched out in two directions at the top. I heard a student whisper to someone who had just joined the cluster, "The *Challenger* blew up. The space shuttle." And the other student said in a hushed whisper, "No way."

Though I may not remember what I did or where I was the day before yesterday, I remember exactly where I was standing when I heard that the space shuttle blew up just after its launch, though that was seventeen years ago now. We all looked up, and have looked up a hundred times since, seeing video replays of that yellow and black explosion, the chaos in the sky, the crosslike shape of the smoke with a fireball at the middle. We can only imagine what happened at the moment when seven brave explorers became martyrs for their cause.

CHRIST LIFTED UP

"I, when I am lifted up from the earth, will draw all men to myself." Of all Jesus' statements that pointed to his cross and what would happen in the world because of his crucifixion, this is one of the most poignant. He said this, according to John, "to show the kind of death he was going to die." Flesh nailed to a crosspiece, hoisted up on a post, hanging in such a way that it was hard to draw a breath. Left to dry, left to die. And all that the people around him could do was to stop and look up. But as they looked up at the torture, they were also looking up toward heaven and the world-changing trans-action that was taking place.

Crowds flowed out of Jerusalem, following the procession out to the "Place of the Skull" as we might follow an ambulance to a smoking heap beside the road. Gapers' block. Hard not to look, hard not to slow down. "The people stood watching . . ." (Luke 23:35).

Jesus' own followers followed him to that place where they did not want to go to. "A large number of people followed him, including women who mourned and wailed for him" (Luke 23:27). They dared not stand too close. "But all those who knew him, including the women who had followed him from Galilee, stood at a distance, watching these things" (Luke 23:49).

Some of those close by participated in the crime, soldiers for whom a crucifixion was one more dirty duty on one more dirty day in the desert so far away from home. "The soldiers also came up and mocked him. They offered him wine vinegar and said, 'If you are the king of the Jews, save yourself'" (Luke 23:36–37).

The authorities who saw the wooden post as a decisive way to lance the boil of Jesus' ministry, to be rid of the problem once and for all, "sneered at him. They said, 'He saved others; let him save himself if he is the Christ of God, the Chosen One'" (Luke 23:35).

We all seek salvation. People use different words for it, but all people, of every place and time, recognize through injury and disappointment and death that something has gone terribly wrong in the world and that we need to be rescued.

So when the soldiers ridiculed Jesus by saying he should save himself from his torture, and when the rulers claimed that the least the Messiah should be able to do is to save himself, and when one of the criminals being crucified next to Jesus taunted, "Aren't you the Christ? Save yourself and us," they all spoke, through bitter, teeth-clenched mouths, of their deep personal need to be saved—but in a way they could barely imagine.

They all looked up. How could they not?

When Jesus was lifted up in that way at that time, he did draw all people to himself. In his book *The Cruciality of the Cross*, P. T. Forsyth wrote, "Christ is to us just what his cross is. All that Christ was in heaven or on earth was put into what he did there. . . . Christ, I repeat, is to us just what his cross is. You do not understand Christ til you understand his cross."

What did Jesus want us to understand about his cross? And why did he "endure the cross, scorning its shame" because of the "joy set before him" (Heb. 12:2)? It was because Jesus knew that when he would be lifted up, he would draw all people to himself.

It is an insult and a source of anguish for Jesus that the human race is broken in so many ways—scattered, disrupted, and alienated. Left in pieces. Something was needed to draw people together, to be reconciled first to God and then to each other. When Jesus was lifted up, when his friends and followers stood stunned, and when even his bitterest enemies focused on his waning life, he became the focal point of all human vision. And we have not been able to look away from the cross since. Think of all the places you see crosses today and consider that even though we do not cringe at its horror when we glance at it up on a church steeple or dangling loosely on a gold chain around a woman's neck, we still choose to focus on it. How can we not?

The crossroad of Golgotha was a great gathering of a scattered humanity. Some walked away no less scattered than before. But a marker had been planted on a hill that would keep us piecemeal people looking toward Jesus and what he did, which was utterly different from what any martyr had ever done. Was he a mock "king of the Jews," as the insulting sign placed above his head said? A Messiah who could not save himself? Or could he truly respond to that dying criminal's request, "Jesus, remember me when you come into your kingdom," with "Today you will be with me in paradise"?

It's hard for us to know how that criminal who died next to Jesus could have had faith in Jesus on that day when Romans soldiers ripped and bloodied him, but the criminal did. He didn't have the advantage we do of seeing Jesus in his death *and* in his resurrection.

TREASURE FROM TOMBS

Howard Carter and a few workmen made their way down an ancient thirty-foot passageway cut into the rock in the Valley of the Kings in Egypt. No human had stepped down that corridor for over three thousand years. At the end of the corridor, Carter began cutting a hole in the door until he was able to peer inside, and there he saw "wonderful things."

Howard had been a sickly and lonely boy in England in the late 1800s, but a visit to an Egyptian exhibit in London had sparked young Howard's imagination. As a young man, he became an artist and landed a job with the Egyptian Exploration Fund as a tracer. He joined Sir Flinders Petrie on an archaeological dig in Egypt and began learning Arabic and the science of digging. In 1900 he was given permission to begin his own dig, and for years he scratched around in the rock and dirt.

Breaking into the chamber, Carter was astonished to be standing among elaborate vases, couches, statues, jewelry, chariots, and a beautiful ostrich-feather fan that stood in perfect condition. The scent of perfume still hung in the air. But then in another chamber came the big surprise: a solid-gold coffin containing the mummified remains of King Tutankhamen, a solid gold mask covering the king's face, with a wreath of flowers on top of it. No one had ever seen a spectacularly rich tomb of an Egyptian king that had gone undiscovered and undisturbed by robbers. And it had all been sealed up in the general era of the great exodus of the Israelites—one of the greatest moments of salvation the world had ever seen.

Tombs are sometimes places of epiphany, but none more so than the one used for Jesus. His tomb was sealed in Jerusalem about fourteen hundred years after young King Tut's. Jesus' tomb was the burial place of one who had been judged a criminal and mocked as a make-believe king. Those who loved Jesus dignified his burial with love and care. His tomb, however, did not remain undisturbed. It was cracked open within days of the burial, but not by human hands. And when first a few women, then a few men, entered, they found . . . absolutely nothing. The grave cloths lay empty and useless. There were no statues or vases or piles of jewelry. No gold. No regal accessories. This tomb was not fit for a king, and it certainly was not fit for the King of Kings, who had no intention of lingering under the false pretense of perfumes.

And yet the emptiness of that tomb held riches none of us can comprehend even now. The power of God—by which Jesus came to life in the tomb, left the tomb, and left the earth in a confident rebuke of all of our greatest enemies, including death—was unleashed in the world.

Now, any of us can choose whether we hope to have enough gold in the tomb to make ourselves comfortable in the coffin or whether we have the vivifying Spirit of Christ filling the decayed parts of our lives and carrying us along with the promise of eternal life.

Look at this phrase: "the unsearchable riches of Christ" (Eph. 3:8). The apostle Paul uses the adjective "unsearchable" here, which means something so great you can't track or trace it. You can't really get your mind around it. It is unsearchable, untraceable, unfathomable, inexhaustible, inscrutable, incalculable, infinite. No matter how much gold you put in a tomb or in a bank account, its measure always has a limit.

But the riches of Christ are beyond all measurement. No scale in the realm of human experience can quantify it. Human love is only a hint of the love of God. Acts of mercy that we read about in the newspaper are just a trickle compared to the flow of mercy that comes from God. Forgiveness is so satisfying when we break open our clutches on someone else and are freed from resentment, but that is just a faint shadow of the forgiveness that God offers us in Christ.

Paul also talks about riches in Ephesians 2: "But because of his great love for us, God, who is rich in mercy, made us alive with Christ even when we were dead in transgressions—it is by grace you have been saved. And God raised us up with Christ and seated us with him in the heavenly realms in Christ Jesus, in order that in the coming ages he might show the incomparable riches of his grace, expressed in his kindness to us in Christ Jesus" (vv. 4–7).

Here's the real promise: if you want to know treasure in life, then realize that it comes from being treasured by God.

About a year ago, I had a few thousand people participate in a survey, and I asked a simple question: If you could ask God one thing, what would it be? Some of the most frequent answers did not surprise me, but one caught my attention: many people wanted to ask God, "Why, why, O God, do you bother to love human beings?" Frankly, I was startled that so many people asked that question.

For all the people who presume God's grace (thinking, "What else, after all, would God do? Isn't love his full-time job?"), there are multitudes who wonder, "Why would God love humans? Why would God love *me*?"

I don't know how to answer that, except to say (as the Bible does) that he just does. Surely the fact that there is no reason, no external necessity, for God to love other than that he chooses to makes his love all the richer and more certain.

Cross and tomb go together in the Christian gospel: both were occupied for a short span, both were abandoned, both were defeated. The apostle Paul, who knew what it was to suffer for choosing to be associated with Jesus, said, "I want to know Christ and the power of his resurrection and the fellowship of sharing in his sufferings, becoming like him in his death" (Phil. 3:10). Paul wrote this when he was in prison and anticipated that his final trial and execution would come at any time. What helped him hold things together, and to hold together the meaning of it all, is that when we are torn to pieces by enemies, we are known by and can know the Lord who was also crushed by his enemies. But on the other side of the apparent defeat is the victory of resurrection.

This applies not just to apostles or to Christians about to be martyred but to every believer who feels that life is too shredded. Evil seems stronger than it should be. Things in life are just getting broken up.

There is no greater promise that God can put the pieces of our lives back together than the resurrection of Jesus. We all know that at the moment of death, a body begins to break down. But Jesus' body did not go through that corruption. The resurrection of Jesus is the greatest miracle, but not because it was so difficult. (Isn't the creation of the universe a larger physical feat? Isn't the conception of human life from two single seeds, from mother and father, a more amazing biological event?) Jesus got up and walked out of his tomb more easily than I got out of bed this morning.

No, the resurrection of Jesus is the greatest miracle because it signifies the greatest truth. The law of entropy, of things falling to pieces, is switched off in the resurrection of Jesus. He would not become dust, and so he proclaimed to us dust creatures that our lives do not need to fall to pieces. The power by which Jesus was raised from the dead brings marriages together, holds us together despite our diverse roles in life, and stops sin from taking us apart like a vicious virus attacking a body.

The Christian gospel tells us to consider the cross and take courage from the empty tomb. Cross and tomb work together; one is incomplete without the other. If Jesus had died only as a martyr for a cause and had not been resurrected, we might have gained inspiration from his death, but not salvation. If Jesus had been brought back to life after having died of natural causes, he would only be an example of miraculous resuscitation, not transformation. But Jesus died a death of salvation and rose from the dead in a transfigured body. Cross and tomb are twin beacons.

BEACONS OF SALVATION

Over the years, I have been interested in lighthouses, probably because Door County, Wisconsin, where I grew up, has many lighthouses around its two-hundred-mile shoreline. There are treacherous shoals around this peninsula, and in the days of wooden ships, hundreds of ships were lost. A great-great-uncle of mine lost his ship on one of the shoals, and I've gone scuba diving on many of the wrecks.

My great-grandfather was the lighthouse keeper at Cana Island Lighthouse, where treacherous autumn Lake Michigan storms beat against it, and my grandmother lived as a child in the lighthouse. I have always seen lighthouses as a vivid symbol of salvation, because I imagine myself in a wooden sailing ship out in the violent waves of a November Lake Michigan storm, heaving a sigh of relief upon sighting a lighthouse and knowing exactly where I am.

In a place called Bailey's Harbor, about halfway up the peninsula, is a different kind of lighthouse. At the shore is a small, white clapboard tower with a light in the top, just twenty feet or so off the ground. The main lighthouse is set back about two hundred yards from the shore. In the stretch between the two lights, the trees have all been cleared so that a boat off the shore can see both lights. This arrangement, called a range light, allows the captain of a boat to find not just the lighthouse but also, when he lines up the two lights, his precise location—and a safe way through the shoals.

The death and resurrection of Jesus are twin beacons; one is incomplete without the other. If you line up the two beacons, you will understand exactly the purpose of Christ's death and the power of his resurrection. Saving sacrifice and triumphant resurrection work together. God is at work on the cross and in the tomb to our benefit.

And so you know exactly where you are.

PRAY THIS

Dear God, I trust you when you say that you love me for no other reason than that it is what you choose. Thank you for loving me in the priceless sacrifice of Jesus. And thank you for loving me by breaking the bonds of death and giving me hope for the future.

FOR REFLECTION OR DISCUSSION

1. What kinds of treasure have you found yourself seeking in order to feel secure in life?
2. What life circumstances have taught you that nothing we can hold in our hands will really satisfy us in life?
3. What specific aspect of God's treasury most motivates you right now: love, mercy, forgiveness, grace?
4. Imagine that you are at the crucifixion of Jesus. What would the experience have been like for you?
5. Can you think of someone whose life was pulled together because he or she was drawn toward the cross of Christ?
6. How might the immense love and grace given in the sacrificial death of Jesus be exactly what you need for today?

Part 3

Living Whole Again

HOW FAITH HAPPENS

14

> Anybody who has been seriously engaged
> in scientific work of any kind realizes
> that over the entrance to the gates
> of the temple of science are written the
> words: Ye must have faith.
> — *Max Planck*

When faith happened in my life, it was like an alluring and irrepressible dawn.

I love watching the sunrise on the horizon of Lake Michigan, and it always reminds me of the dawning of the new life of faith. The black-painted sky gradually thins, and stars lose their sparkle against the graying morning. On the horizon, where the sun hides low like a lion in tall grass, the darkness melts before the advancing red-tinged light. A fire is coming. And then it shoots out across the landscape, just a small ray, but the darkness has no chance against it. Then the brilliant arch advances. By the time the full orb rides on the horizon, its radiant heat is already drying the night air and warming my face.

Others would say that faith happened to them in a more muted and overcast, but no less genuine, way. It was still the birth of day after the night. I say "happen" because it is foolish for us to think that we initiate faith or define it or shape it. When I became a believer in a dramatic new way at the age of seventeen, it was like being irradiated by a power over which I had no control and which compelled me to believe. I was able to tell people, "I *really* believe in God now," not with any sense that I had done anything, or read the right book, or talked to the right person, or been in the right place. It would be foolish to brag that you believe in the sun. No, you believe because it is so obvious.

FAITH CONNECTS US WITH THE TRUSTWORTHY CREATOR

It is extraordinarily hard to live without faith because we were created to be trusting creatures—and in that trust to be connected with the altogether trustworthy Creator. Without faith, you cannot call somebody else a friend, and the thought would never cross your mind to call God your friend.

Faith is never a matter of proofs and statistics. For example, I believe my wife loves me. I know that to be a fact. Yet I can't tell you the exact date on which that faith came alive in me. I can't give you a list of empirical evidence that proves her love. I could list examples of that love—instances of compassion, understanding, support, joy. But my trust that she does love me comes not from a ceiling-high stack of evidence but somehow from the core of one person to another.

At its heart, that's the way faith in God works. There is, of course, evidence of his existence and his love and power, but all kinds of people look at that same body of evidence, and some conclude there is a loving God and others conclude there is not.

Faith is born in a person's inner being; it is not simply a decision. Faith is a dynamic relationship, not just a stack of assertions.

People of faith who believe that God is real and that he is alive and active in the world have simply registered in a conscious way that a brilliant light has overwhelmed them. Like a new day dawning, they realize that they have awakened, even if they don't know exactly when the waking started.

CERTAIN OF WHAT WE DO NOT SEE

Here is one definition of faith: "Faith is being sure of what we hope for and certain of what we do not see" (Heb. 11:1). Faith is not a catalog of things we know because we have accumulated knowledge of them through our eyes or ears or touch; it is the knowledge of things that can slip past the eyes, that are sometimes mere whispers in the ear or a brush on the shoulder. When the disciple Thomas went down on his knees upon seeing the resurrected Jesus and voiced the absolute statement of trust, "My Lord and my God!" Jesus replied, "Because you have seen me, you have believed; blessed are those who have not seen and yet have believed" (John 20:28–29). So on the one hand, there is the evidence of things that "we have seen with our eyes, which we have looked at and our hands have touched," as the disciple John put it regarding his experience with Jesus. Then there is faith that reaches across a distance and stands on truth. Blessed are those who believe in the God who is beyond our eyes but whose works flood our vision every day.

When my daughter was a baby and my wife would put her in my arms and leave the room, the baby's head would shift, her eyes would scan back and forth, her brow would wrinkle, and then—most certainly—came that cry of distress. A cry that cut to the quick. I knew she was thinking, "Mom has disappeared. She is gone. She has ceased to exist. And I will never ever see her again." A baby does not have the cognitive ability to know that someone continues to exist even when the physical evidence is withdrawn. Babies cannot be "certain of what we do not see."

But give the kid a couple of years, and he or she will understand that the doorway to the next room is not a monster's mouth swallowing up the next person to pass that way. The child will even come to understand that Mom or Dad can be in Cincinnati or Los Angeles or London and still exist and, more important, that they still exist in relationship. Not being visible is not the same as not being. And sometimes a relationship is even stronger when there is some distance.

REASON AND FAITH

To be human is to believe, holding in your consciousness a whole galaxy of realities that includes the visible and the invisible. Not to believe, or being unwilling to believe, or thinking that believing is far too much to ask, is to tear out the heart of who we were made to be. It is to limit life to a kind of closet where facts are sorted on hangers and racks, instead of living life in wide-open spaces that connect to unseen reality.

Some people think that one of the great debates in life is whether you are going to live your life by reason or by faith.

The reason-only way of life says, "I can base my life only on the tangible, visible, measurable facts of life—as my reason sorts them out. My belief is in data; empirical conclusions are my creed. There is no truth apart from physical facts, so I don't need to worry about the taboos and codes of people across the river from me, and I will certainly never impose any morality on them. To live is to be a real-ist, so I will not believe in what I cannot see, and I will not chase a God who obviously cannot be known." This is, for its proponents, the sensible way to live. Sensible because it is based on senses.

The faith-only way of life can be equally risky. It says, "I choose to be skeptical of all evidence. I will assume that most good beliefs are beyond rationality and will almost always seem irrational. Faith is inherently subjective, as it should be. Therefore, I experience faith, I believe what I choose to believe, and I don't believe faith has any accountability to anyone or anything else—least of all to a body of supposed 'facts.' It doesn't matter if my faith contradicts the faith of the guy next door, because we all have a right to our own faith. Faith is more like dreams than data."

But there is a third option.

Most people realize that everything we know of life, and every-thing God points us to, assumes that life is a matter of faith *and* rea-son. Sometimes I come to believe something that I have come to understand. And often I come to understand something that I have come to believe first. But there is one reality, and in the end the facts will line up with faith.

What about the question of doubt? You cannot talk about believing without talking about doubt any more than you can talk about day without implying night. Some people think faith is an all-or-nothing proposition. "You had better believe in God," these people maintain, "and everything that God says, because if you show any hesitation, any gap, any questioning, he will look at you with a scowl and snatch away from you the whole blessing."

No. God is not a troll beneath a bridge, expecting us to give all the right answers to riddles he poses before we can cross. God is not the examiner at the Department of Motor Vehicles, mindlessly administering the same test a million times, requiring a 90 percent to pass.

What we see in the Bible time and again are people of great faith who live on the border of where faith stops and where hesitation begins.

Faith Rises on the Horizon of Doubt

On and off over the years I've had the pleasure of teaching students in theology classes, and those classes tend to take on different personalities. I remember one class that was dominated by lively, energetic believers who were always pushing me ahead, always asking the questions that were just a step or two beyond my preparation. They were smart enough to know when I tried passing off an answer as being simpler than it was. Another class was dominated by dull, listless people who would rarely rise to the occasion of engaged discussion. It probably was my fault for never discovering the connecting points that would coax them out of their shells. But the kind of class that has been the most challenging and fulfilling for me was the class well-sprinkled with doubting Thomases. They were in the class not because they had full faith but because they were seeking it. They weren't afraid to stare blankly if my response to a question just wasn't adding up.

Why is it that we consider the rising sun on the horizon, spilling its light across the land, an event of note but not the sun sitting brilliantly above at high noon? It's because the horizon is a line where something new crosses over. And so doubt is not really the antithesis of faith; it is its precursor.

Even when Jesus' own disciples had the extraordinary experience of speaking with him after his resurrection, on top of a rocky Galilean mountain, while some worshiped him, "some doubted" (literally, "hesitated"). If the risen Christ passed *you* on the sidewalk, or even entered the room where you are at this very moment, it would not mean that all your doubts in life would disappear in an instant. You would still have to believe.

Faith is a *calling*. It is backed up by a universe of tangible facts about the goodness and greatness of God. Yet faith is still an outward extension of trust, so that we are certain of what we do not see.

Faith is a *process*. Believing is a flow of relationship, back and forth, a continual conversation of a person and the Person. That's why faith builds over time. The conversation courses back and forth; you go over old topics you've shared with God as well as new subjects, questions you never would have thought to ask years ago. But with each declaration we make to God, whether it's thanks or praise or pain or anguish, that link gets stronger. And when we listen to God, the certainty that he is there in all of his greatness and goodness becomes firm ground beneath our feet.

For most people, the process of belief building doesn't happen along a completely smooth, upward path. Building a relationship is not like building an automobile, in which each part must be put in place in order, by the laws of physical objects. More like a child-parent affinity, belief may surge ahead with new insights and convictions, but it may also get bogged down, slowed so that it looks motionless, or may even seem on the slide. We may have fits of temper when we stomp our feet and declare that we will *not* believe, like a teenager asserting independence. Or we may race down a faith road that is off course, only to find ourselves confused and retracing our steps—if we are wise about it. On our best days, believing is like a walk—steady, progressive, full of considered sensation. It may be the walk of friends or the march of the soldier into some battleground of life. Our steps toward God are sometimes lunging and at other times running, creeping, or stumbling. Style is not the issue, and it's better to fall toward God than away from him. Put one foot in front of the other, and you'll be moving toward the destination.

Faith is an *invitation*. For all the teaching that Jesus did, from one village to the next in Galilee and among the imposing pillars of Solomon's portico at the temple in Jerusalem, it all boils down to this: believe. Which is not to say believe in anything you choose. It is an invitation to believe the realities that Jesus explained as meticulously as a carpenter carving and piecing together wood to make the furniture of life. It is to believe him, and in him—and in the believing, to gain the right to become children of God.

PRAY THIS

God, I want to believe. Help me in my unbelief.

FOR REFLECTION OR DISCUSSION

1. What are you certain of?
2. What do you find easy to believe about God and his ways, and what is more difficult for you to believe?
3. If you were tempted to lean toward the faith-only way of life or the reason-only way of life, which would it be? Why?
4. How do you think you would have responded if you had talked with Jesus after his resurrection?
5. If you were to ask God to strengthen your faith in any particular way right now, what would that be?

BELIEF
AND AUTHORITY

15

> If you wish to know what a man is,
> place him in authority.
> — *Yugoslavian proverb*

I don't remember how or why, but when I was thirteen years old, I went with a couple of buddies to a political rally in my hometown for a candidate for president of the United States. I'm sure it was for the novelty of it, since I had no commitment to any candidate. But he was a candidate for *that* office. He wanted to become the most powerful man in the world. "I should see this in person at least once," I thought. I had never seen a room full of that kind of enthusiasm before, rivaling even a stadium full of football fans. Huge red, white, and blue banners shouted the candidate's name from all four sides of the room. The emotional windup of the program was like riding up the steep incline of a roller coaster, storing energy for the big rush. And then the candidate emerged. He stepped into the brilliant wash of the spotlight and up to the podium, where he spoke out to the crowd the core of his convictions, building to shouting at the end. The power of one voice and one microphone was astonishing.

One of the boldest things any human being can do is to stand in front of someone else and say, "*This* is what I *believe*." We listen, whether we are inclined to believe the same thing or not.

Belief in God and in the truths of God is a distinctive experience. It is to say, "I have come to a certain conviction. I have listened, I have watched, I have thought about it. I now believe I know something I did not know before. And it isn't so much that I have chosen to believe as that belief has been born in me by a reality greater than myself. I have a sense of certitude, and my next steps in life will be different for it. I am carried along by this truth."

Many people today think that belief in this sense is not possible anymore, that we know better than that now. To say you believe in something or someone absolutely is to be certain where there is no certainty. It is to risk being a social pariah, because to say you absolutely know something will prove antisocial to at least somebody along the way. One thing is certain, these people say: be suspicious of certainty. And they are quite certain about this uncertainty.

THE THING WE BELIEVE IS LARGER THAN OURSELVES

But belief is not about us. The true believer doesn't focus on himself, saying, "*I* believe this." Rather, he or she says, "I believe *this*." The more we focus on the experience of believing, the greater the risk that we can believe something just for the sake of believing.

Belief is not just about knowing; it is about trusting. True faith in God is one of the most intimate states a person can experience. It is not just about gathering and processing information; otherwise a computer would be a "believer" of sorts. Because there is so much information to process, so many voices to listen to, so many topics that get thrown in our faces every day, we use up most of our "belief energy" just sorting it all out. In the contemporary world, believing becomes a matter of calculating and drawing a sum. We forget that the most important belief in life is a decision not about *what* but about *whom*. Faith says, *this* God I can trust.

When we believe, when we trust, we are the most human we ever are, because we are actively connecting with our Creator, anchoring ourselves in his unchangeable nature. Knowing and trusting a friend or a spouse projects us into a world larger than ourselves—how much more so when we know and trust the God who made us and who loves us with an irrepressible love.

But whom should we believe? And why? Which God? Which religion? Which doctrine?

STUNNED BY THE UNEXPECTED

Have you ever had the experience of being outdoors somewhere, turning a corner, and being stunned by a scene you were not expecting, nor could have imagined?

Years ago my wife and I were hiking in a beautiful place in the Scottish highlands called Glen Nevis. The narrow green valley was pleasant as we followed a stream, looking up the mossy rock sides of the mountains. But then we turned a corner, far along enough on the trail to be alone, and the valley lay like a green carpet, with the biggest mountain at the end and a single silvery ribbon waterfall tracing down the mountain. We realized that the sound of the waterfall had been slowly growing in volume as we walked the path, but we weren't expecting that thin tower of water, sparkling and spectacular.

Another time, when we took our children on a family trip to the Grand Canyon, I didn't realize how close we were. The land was flat along the road we followed. Signs read, "GRAND CANYON," but I couldn't see anything grand at all. We saw a parking spot at a viewing station, pulled the car over, and went to the railing. There below us was an amazing alien world. A vast sunken cavity in which people that looked like specks hiked along the ridges and shelves going deeper into the crevasse. It was like stumbling into a whole other world. One of my kids expressed astonishment, summing it all up in the simplest way: "Man, that's *big*." I couldn't resist. "Yes, *maybe* that's why they call it the *Grand* Canyon!" They looked at me with that bemused look that says, "Yes, this is the kind of comment we teenagers have to put up with on family vacations."

Time and again people responded to Jesus' words with speechless astonishment. Perhaps as they listened to Jesus' teaching, they occasionally found themselves turning a corner and being stunned by a vista of reality that was bigger and grander than they had imagined. Not everyone who heard Jesus became believers; we all have personal agendas that can hold us in disbelief. But everyone who heard Jesus speak had to grapple with the power of what he said, and they had to decide what to do with the authoritative voice with which he spoke—an authority that came not from a booming microphone or spotlights or banners but from the ring of truth in the words themselves, which were backed up by every action he performed.

The gospel writers make it clear that one of the outstanding features of Jesus' ministry was that he exercised this authority freely and naturally. People sensed they were under the immediate influence of God. Jesus' words struck at the heart; they were clear, strong, unequivocal, simple, and mysterious. They both wounded and healed, and when they did wound, they offered immediate healing as well. His words still stick in people's minds, and they keep moving across the landscape of history like a cyclone. That's why almost everybody, including even proponents of other religions, show respect for the thunder and lightning of Jesus' teaching.

RESPECT AND RESPONSE

But showing respect is one thing; responding is another. In the Sermon on the Mount, Jesus talked about one man who built his house on a rock foundation and another man whose house rested on a bed of unstable sand. The house-on-sand person only hears Jesus' words, whereas the house-on-rock person hears and practices. Respect plus response. Right after this tale of two builders, Matthew mentions the people's astonishment at Jesus' authority. The people were not saying, "Did you hear what this fellow is trying to assert?" They were swept up in the power of the Word himself. His authority carried them, and it carries us still. It summons us not just to listen but to act.

House building is a metaphor for life. Christ does not assert authority so that he can push his weight around. God doesn't impose commands so that he can have a bevy of mindless followers. His is an act of grace. These authoritative words come to us because God knows there is so much we need to learn about life. Ignorance may not be a sin, but it is an extraordinarily dangerous way to live.

When someone asks, "Why should I believe what Christianity teaches?" or, "Why should I believe the specific things taught about personal ethics, life after death, God's providence in history, angels, and failure?" the answer he or she deserves is that followers of Jesus Christ believe such things (knowing *and* trusting) because they believe they have heard an authoritative voice on the matters. Christ summons, and the oracles of prophets and the writings of apostles are *Holy* Scripture—the exhalation of God's own Spirit.

I participated once in a discussion with someone about psychic knowledge, and the person commented, "I could believe that." I wondered, "What does she mean, 'I could believe that'?" Thinking "I could believe that" is a short step from saying "I want to believe that," which is one more short step from "I choose to believe that." "But why believe something just because you think you could?" I wondered. Isn't the question, *Should* I believe that?

That is why we need authority.

I could believe that there was once a land called Atlantis; the romanticism and mystery of it is titillating. I could believe it just because I want to believe it. I could believe that intelligent beings from other galaxies are living in my community right now. (I can even think of a few likely names.) I could believe that cancer is caused by cold winters because someone once wrote a book claiming that. But what *should* I believe? Shouldn't my beliefs line up with reality?

Frighteningly, many people today don't care whether their beliefs line up with reality. If their beliefs have a pleasing or useful effect in life, they go ahead and hold on to them. They don't worry about whether the beliefs are grounded in truth or not. It's too much of a hassle to conform beliefs to the form of reality, and it's certainly inconvenient to risk conflict with someone else's beliefs. Besides, these people ask, is there any such thing as truth anyway?

But we all know, really, that we can't live that way. We *don't* live that way. When we receive a bank statement on our accounts, we assume that the transactions line up with the reality of our actual deposits and withdrawals. In fact, we assume that they line up precisely, that the balance is not a whimsical number a bank official decided to put on the statement. When someone is on trial for murder, we assume that the careful process of deliberation will produce a verdict that is true. If a doctor tells you he believes a growth in your abdomen is completely benign and thus does not require surgery, you want to know that this is not an arbitrary opinion on his part because his schedule is too booked to fit in another surgery. You don't want the doctor thinking, "I *could* believe it's benign."

But, some will argue, it is different with religious beliefs because they are not as objective as legal and medical and financial matters. We shouldn't go looking for religious authority, because no one should dare to call anybody else wrong or have the audacity to say that they have found spiritual truth.

But if we're honest, we've got to say there really is a Creator or there isn't.

Says Who?—Says God

The issue of authority always comes back to the matter of *who* rather than *what*. Who is this oncologist I'm going to see? Who is this political pundit offering a comprehensive analysis of conflicts in the Middle East? Who is this person asking me to vote for him or her for political office?

Do you remember when you were a kid and someone told you something you resisted or doubted? How often we would reply, "Says who?" And we especially said, "Says who?" when someone was asserting some kind of authority over us.

It always comes back to the same place: "Who?" Almost anybody can be right once in a while, which is why the search for truth isn't based on a *what*. As someone once said, even a broken clock is correct twice a day.

But if you find the right *who*, the person who is right not just by accident or by passing fair judgment but because truth is at the core of that person's being, then you've found proper authority in life.

Now, here is the best part about acknowledging God as the absolute authority over all matters of truth: God pulls all the pieces of belief together. The reality of God, of the human race, of the natural world, of good and evil, of purpose, all fits together to make a house you can live in. If you pick up a book about French or about maintaining your car or about building an airplane, you assume page 12 will not contradict page 98. One part of the book will not deny what another part has asserted. If one author has written the book, with one intent and consistent knowledge, the body of information he offers is a harmonious whole.

Christianity does not offer bits and scraps of disconnected truths or mere sentiments. If one thing is true—really and unalterably true—it fits with all the other truths we pick up as pieces along the way, and an amazing picture emerges. And this knowledge does not contradict scientific knowledge. A good astrophysicist and a good theologian are really doing the same thing: passionately seeking to discover the way things really are. What they pick up along the way may sometimes seem to pull in different directions, but ultimately what is true is true. And it all fits.

Pray This

Lord, help me to trust that what you say is absolutely true. Allow me in the weeks to come to have an experience with your words in Scripture that instructs, informs, inspires, and guides me. May your Word be a bright light shining on my path. And when I, in my stubborn way, think that I know better than you, please guide me back to the safe harbor of your truth.

For Reflection or Discussion

1. What is your natural reaction to God being the authority over life? Comfort? Resistance? Certainty? Skepticism?

2. Why would some people who say they believe in a divine Creator of all things not be inclined to consider that he has authority in their lives?
3. What are the consequences if we think that one person can believe one body of truths and another can hold to a completely contradictory set of truths?

WHAT THE STARS SAY

16

> Science has proof
> without any certainty.
> Creationists have certainty
> without any proof.
> — *Ashley Montague*

It was a cold December night, as I recall, when my best friend, Roger, and I went with the local astronomy club, a group of seasoned adult stargazers, out into a frosty field, where we pointed binoculars and telescopes up into the black sky salted with stars. For Roger and me, both twelve years old at the time, recognizing constellations was fascinating. We learned the difference between stars, which glittered, and planets, which glowed with a steadier light. We pointed my mail-order telescope at a star, and that point of light became—well, actually, just a slightly larger point of light (the biggest disappointment of a magical evening). But then we panned across the plains and mountains of the moon, seeing it magnified as a real place, a real but alien world in real time. The silence in that field (why we were whispering, I'm not sure) made that examination of the moon the more mysterious, like we were looking into someone else's private world—more like spies than scientists. It was almost as if we were waiting for some undiscovered life-form to walk across the moonscape.

But the most important thing that happened that night, which I recall every time I'm out in the country under a great bowl of sky, was that overwhelming sense of the universe's immensity.

Or, to use a far better word, the creation.

CREATION: THE WHOLE THING

Universe, after all, means "the whole thing." It is shorthand for every world, every speck of cosmic dust, every rock, every four-legged creature, every human being, every gamma ray and photon that exist anywhere. Put it all together and you have "universe."

It was God who put it all together. He fashioned it. He conceived it and then willed it into being. "Let there be light," he said, "and there was light." We all know the opening words of the Bible: "In the beginning God created the heavens and the earth." The Hebrew word for *create* does not mean merely the rearrangement of matter. It is not the idea of a potter shaping clay or a woodworker building a cabinet. No construction worker ever said, "Let there be iron." To create, in the most fundamental sense, means to bring into existence.

From Aristotle to the twentieth century, people have thought that the universe is eternal, or at least that the stuff of which it is made has always existed. Then twentieth-century astrophysicists began seeing in the stars evidence of a distinct beginning, a time when the very existence of the universe began, which is hard for us to imagine. But that is both the emerging scientific consensus today and the clear assertion of Scripture: "By faith we understand that the universe was formed at God's command, so that what is seen was *not* made out of what was *visible*" (Heb. 11:3, italics mine).

CREATION FROM NOTHING

Something out of nothing.

Is it a stretch for us to believe there is a being who can create something out of nothing? Of course it is. In fact, it is more than a stretch, because our minds can't conceive of God's greatness. And if someone says, "Yes, that is always the line religious people take— God is beyond our understanding," an appropriate reply is, "Yes, that is the meaning of God, and if God were small enough to fit into our comprehension entirely, he would be far too diminutive to create anything in the first place or to recreate it now."

Countless people have said that when they experienced some utterly hopeless situation, God brought something out of it. Because he is the Creator, there is always hope that utterly new and unexpected things can happen.

Because the creation came out of nothing (*ex nihilo*), everything that exists comes from God's creative act, though the corruptions and sicknesses that have crept in since then are not his creation. This is very important. God did not and cannot create evil. God is not in favor of corruption. He doesn't like animosity or war or cancer. That is the way things have become, but it is not the way things were created.

What, then, did God create?

"By him all things were created: things in heaven and on earth, visible and invisible, whether thrones or powers or rulers or authorities; all things were created by him and for him. He is before all things, and in him all things hold together" (Col. 1:16–17). This passage is speaking about Christ, making the point that the Son of God was present and involved when the universe was willed into existence. "All things." Every physical reality and every spiritual reality exists because God created it.

In a mighty song at the beginning of the book of Revelation, four "living creatures" bearing the looks of a lion, an ox, a man, and an eagle—covered with eyes, fitted with wings, moving about a throne before a sea of glass, focusing day and night on proclaiming the holiness of God—these four creatures representing the whole of creation, sing these words:

> You are worthy, our Lord and God,
> to receive glory and honor and power,
> for you created all things,
> and by your will they were created
> and have their being.
>
> —Revelation 4:11

The whole creation—not just us sometimes miserable human beings—waits and longs for God's healing and redemptive acts. "The whole creation has been groaning as in the pains of childbirth" (Rom. 8:22), looking for the day when God will free us from decay and disease and disruption and bring us back to the way we were when created.

In the meantime, we look up into the sky and are appropriately awed. So many worlds, such vast distances, such resplendent and unabashed beauty. It is all there in the lights that burn and glitter, in the bloom of supernovas, in galaxies full of billions of stars, whose radiating arms spin undetectably within the span of a human lifetime.

> The heavens declare the glory of God;
> > the skies proclaim the work of his hands.
> Day after day they pour forth speech;
> > night after night they display knowledge.
> There is no speech or language
> > where their voice is not heard.
> Their voice goes out into all the earth,
> > their words to the ends of the world.
> > > —PSALM 19:1–4

That is what the stars say.

But the creation is not just up there. We are standing on it, and in it, and among it. You've never met a person who is not an intentional act of God's creation. Look in the mirror; you too are an intentional act of God. You stand with hundreds of species of vertebrates and invertebrates, with mirror mountain lakes, and with the angels. All created. All the will of God.

TAKE A GOOD LOOK AT YOURSELF

But what do you really see when you look in the mirror? You probably notice the lines that were not there a year ago. The scar just beneath your chin from when you went headfirst over your bicycle when you were a kid and they stitched you up with little thought to cosmetic effect. Your eye is drawn to your retreating hairline or your sagging skin. Your eyes have seen the pleasing and the ugly. You may even look at your face in the mirror and wonder, as we all do, "Is that really who I am?" Not because of the flaws but because you know that your soul is too big to be circumscribed in a face.

But this would be a good thing to think when you look in the mirror: creation. God chose me to be. And whether I feel well-connected right now or terribly estranged, I really am part of a vast creative work. It isn't just God and me in the world. I'm part of a whole. If this is a good day because good things happen, it's not just a day for me to feel good. It is the hand of the Creator moving across the plane in which I live. And if this is a bad day because bad things happen, it is probably because this whole thing that I'm part of, this universe, this fabric, has stresses and strains on it all the time. It all fits together, but some days it falls to pieces.

If you believe in "God the Father Almighty, Maker of heaven and earth," if you believe that "in the beginning, God created the heavens and the earth" out of the darkness and the void, that will determine the basic structure of your life. This is the genesis. It is *your* genesis. It is the first flash of subatomic energy, the first explosion of real matter, and the first breath of the first living creature. It is the moment your mother's egg and father's seed join and a complete set of chromosomes, the pattern of your genetic self, is established.

PUTTING TOGETHER THE PIECES OF CREATION

If you believe in the creation, you will also say:

1. *To understand my life, and my purpose in life, I need to go continually back to God.* He is the designer. He is the artisan. He had intent. We need to understand it. Because we are here by God's act of creation and not by accident, we bear an honor and a responsibility. We are part of a larger community; we are stewards of a vast world. We are not just one more species of carnivore trying to get a bigger hunk of meat than the next carnivore. We are to serve as the conscience of the earth.

2. *My life cannot have been an accident.* The starkest theory of evolutionary development proposes that if enough time passes (tens of millions of years) and enough random mutations in a species occur (with natural selection guaranteeing the favorable mutations will survive), then a single-cell organism can eventually yield a human being. This idea of life's development is the best theory available *if* you assume no supernatural creator. And that is what some scientists and philosophers feel that they need to do. They have to explain the empirical universe solely in empirical terms because any idea of God has to do with religious experience, which they classify as a category of knowledge (or as not being knowledge at all) that is so far removed from the real world that it cannot be brought alongside the conclusions of natural science.

But the assumption that the possible existence of a Creator has nothing to do with the knowledge we have about the natural world is a huge one. What about the scientists today who say that the universe appears to have an element of design? Why can't the possibility of a Creator be calculated into the possible scenarios of how this universe came to be? (Someone has said that the mathematical chances of an intelligent life-form emerging from random chance is the same as the chances that letters strewn from an airplane will fall on the ground in the form of a Shakespeare play.)

No, here is where faith begins. "I believe in God the Father Almighty, Maker . . ." You are not an accident. You are not merely the best mutation in the neighborhood. You are not merely a species who is really good at avoiding getting eaten by another species. You can seek design and purpose in your life because you were created according to a design. And a "very good" one at that.

3. *My life can glorify God.* Creation's loud speech, that wordless praise, is the song my life is meant to sing. I know how far from the glory of God I fall short. I know how entangled and entrapped my life can become. I know how off-key is the song of my life. But somehow it is possible for my life to offer one more speech directed to the great and the good, to join in the chorus with the stars. To glorify God means to believe that your life can point to his substantial goodness and righteousness. It means that your life can fit with all

kinds of other pieces of truth that contribute to the great truth, the great reality that a glorious God decided to create the dust of the unformed universe, out of which he would create stars and planets and beagles and fish and human beings. This is the truth, the unassailable truth: there is more than us. We are not the biggest and the best. We come from a master artisan who had a master design and who is still shaping the stuff of our lives. I will seek God's help for that to happen.

4. *Nothing that exists was made evil.* If God is great and God is good, it is impossible for him to create sin or wickedness. He did not and does not create the malevolent or the immoral. Somehow things got spoiled. Things that were whole got cracked and fell to pieces. God began the creation with "Let there be light" and the darkness was filled, but in the history of the world, the light keeps getting turned off and the shadows take over—but only for a while.

In the beginning God created the land and the seas and said, "It is good." Then he created the plants and trees, "and God saw that it was good." The two great lights in the sky—good. The great creatures of the sea, every winged bird, livestock, reptiles—good, good, good. And when it was all done, when God finally placed someone like himself in the world, a creature of clay and spirit—like God, able to sense the right, sentient, intentional, and spiritually perceptive—then God stood back from it all and pronounced it not just good but "very good."

Context Shapes Identity

What the stars say matters because we all shape how we view ourselves by the context of where we live, who and what surrounds us, and whose voice we listen to. Context shapes identity.

If you grow up in an African-American home, or in an Amish community, or in Brooklyn, you will pick up a view of the world and of yourself as surely as you will gain an accent. The schools you attend will indoctrinate you, no matter what their stated intention is. Your church will indoctrinate you too and may even overtly state that that's its purpose. But with all these voices telling us who we are and how we should think, if we miss the big context, the voice of creation itself, we will have neglected one of the main ways in which God defines us and shapes our lives.

A community of ants living in an anthill could believe that that hill—the mass of teeming bodies of other ants, scurrying about looking for food, dragging twigs, and moving grains of sand—constitutes the whole world. But what a tiny world. It's not "the whole thing."

Human beings should know better. Our context is not just our subculture. It is not just the tribe we belong to or the nation we live in. And it's not even just the human race. Pull back, way back. Wind that wide-angle lens back as far as it will go to encompass the full extent of what God's Word tells us, and we will see that we are part of this universe, this creation. And why does that matter? It matters because your fundamental identity as a human being begins with your creatureliness, your createdness. Being fully alive means being able to start the day with the conscious realization that the Almighty, the Benevolent, the Artisan, brought you into existence, and he placed you in the middle of his garden called Earth, in the middle of a continual fireworks-like display called the universe. There is nothing in this masterpiece that does not belong, and nothing is missing that should be. The pieces make a whole. As your day progresses and you get slammed by someone you trusted, or get a phone call with ominous news, or slip yourself into the wheelchair that has been your prison (or chariot) for years, you can know that even in that moment, the heavens are declaring the glory of the Creator and that the earth will not be silenced. You can know that the least note you sound in acknowledgment of the Creator blends with the harmony that has been the music of ages past and will be for all of eternity.

PRAY THIS

Lord, give me a wider view. Help me to see the parts of the cre-
ation that are groaning as if in childbirth, but help me also to see
the exuberant, exultant, light-filled glory that issues from you and
gives this universe, and me in it, a dignity that can come from
nowhere else.

FOR REFLECTION OR DISCUSSION

1. When was the last time you heard the "voice" of creation calling out the glory of God, as described in Psalm 19?
2. Read the creation account in the first two chapters of Genesis. What things do you observe that you haven't noticed before?
3. What questions do you have about how you as a human being fit into God's creation?
4. How are human beings to be stewards of the earth? What is the spiritual value in this?
5. Why are some people much more inclined to see the universe as a random accident than as a creation?
6. How do you think you can more fully take in the truths revealed to us in the creation?

FINDING PEACE
WITH GOD

> My good friends, for the second time in our
> history, a British Prime Minister has returned
> from Germany bringing peace with honour.
> I believe it is peace for our time. . . .
> Go home and get a nice quiet sleep.
> — *British Prime Minister Neville Chamberlain,*
> *after meeting with Adolf Hitler in 1938*

Last summer I was watching my sixteen-year-old daughter walk around inside the great temple-like Lincoln Memorial in Washington, D.C., and when she stood under the massive inscription of Lincoln's second inaugural address on the inside north wall, with the stern stone statue of Lincoln behind us, looking out across the capital, I had a flashback to fourteen years earlier when she and I had stood in the same spot. In diapers then, she had trotted along the stone floor, fascinated by the slap-slap sounds her shoes made. I was reading the inscription, words written by a president weary of the bloodstain of years of civil war and hoping that the nightmare of national enmity might be nearing an end: "With malice toward none, with charity for all, with firmness in the right as God gives us to see the right, let us strive on to finish the work we are in, to bind up the nation's wounds, to care for him who shall have borne the battle and for his widow and orphan, to do all which may achieve and cherish a just and lasting peace. . . ."

As I read, my diapered girl ran back and forth with glee on the stone beneath the thirty-foot-high inscription. Then another kid about her age, who happened to be African American, joined her. I looked at the words, the white kid, the black kid, back at the words, back at the kids. I brought my camera to my eye, lining up the viewfinder so that the children appeared as two small sprites beneath the massive inscription. And then (I'm not kidding) they happened to meet and gave each other a hug! Right there, beneath *those* words. With my finger on the shutter, I thought, "*Life* magazine, *Life* magazine." I clicked the shutter.

No film.

On that March day in 1865 when President Lincoln gave this short speech, the weather was foul. It had rained for weeks in Washington, turning Pennsylvania Avenue into a sea of mud. The crowd stood in the muck at the base of the Capitol's steps, its stately new dome one sign of hope that the nation might actually survive its trauma. Journalist Noah Brooks was there and reported that as Lincoln got up from his seat, "a roar of applause shook the air, and, again and again repeated, finally dying away on the outer fringe of the throng, like a sweeping wave upon the shore." Then, Brooks says, "just at that moment the sun, which had been obscured all day, burst forth in its unclouded meridian splendor and flooded the spectacle with glory and with light." The journalist noted that Lincoln later said to him, "Did you notice that sunburst? It made my heart jump."

The crowd listened in profound silence. The words no doubt planted themselves in the people's consciousness immediately, tense and poignant as those late Civil War days were. But, according to Brooks, "chiefly memorable in the mind of those who saw that second inauguration must still remain the tall, pathetic, melancholy figure of the man who, then inducted into office in the midst of the glad acclaim of thousands of people, and illumined by the deceptive brilliance of a March sunburst, was already standing in the shadow of death."

Within weeks, Lincoln would be shot dead.

"With malice toward none, with charity for all, let us strive to do all which may achieve and cherish a just and lasting peace."

SEARCHING FOR A PLACE OF PEACE

I talk to people all the time whose main search in life is for one simple thing: a place of peace. They would welcome a whole day without fighting in their home. They would be thrilled to get through a week of work without feeling beat up. Might a cabin provide that place of peace? A boat? Some unclaimed corner of the house? But most people realize that the place of peace must reside in the heart. For however many external storms there are, and however hard the lightning snaps and the mud grabs at your feet, the battle is really inside.

Here are words worthy of a twenty-foot-high stone inscription (no, let's say one hundred or two hundred feet high): "For God was pleased to have all his fullness dwell in [Christ], and through him to reconcile to himself all things, whether things on earth or things in heaven, by *making peace* through his blood, shed on the cross" (Col. 1:19–20, italics mine).

God knows, he really knows, just how intense the wars on earth are. Civil wars are the massacre of civil brotherhood, but God knows that they too kill humanity—the dismemberment of Adam. I've talked to many people who have been robbed or raped or attacked, and they always talk about the utter and complete violation of self that occurred, and that is why they sleep fitfully. To God, it is that plus a desecration of the sanctuary that is a human person. When an evil deed despoils a human person, it is like spilling blood in a temple. No wonder we want peace. No wonder God wants peace.

We want peace not just because we want to stop the bruising and the beating. You don't have peace in your life if you can merely write in your diary at the end of the day, "Thank God, nobody beat me up today." If a husband and wife stop bickering but still live in the ice-cold atmosphere of indifference, that isn't exactly peace.

PEACE, THE TRANQUILITY OF ORDER

Peace has to do with order, "the tranquility of order," as Augustine called it so many centuries ago. It means living in the reality of the way things truly stack up in life—as God defines life. Ordered peace is like the security a child senses from parents who draw clear boundaries by appropriately saying no and yes. Peace comes from the ordering of the pieces of life—top things on top, and on down from there.

That means seeing God as *the* top. It means letting the high things shape the lower things. It is a boyfriend treating his girlfriend on the basis of principle and not just hormones. It is being a citizen and not just a consumer. It is being a reconciler and not just a competitor.

The harsh truth of the matter, though, is that the kind of peace that is "just and lasting" often comes through suffering. We ought to have freely relinquished slavery, but we had to war over it. Lincoln should have gotten his statue without the bullet.

And peace on earth should have been possible without the blood of the beautiful Shepherd, but that is the way peace came. "Peace through his blood, shed on the cross." Everything within us wants to deny that we have ever lived at odds with God. How can that possibly be? "Some misbehavior here and there on our part surely is not the same thing as aggression toward God," we think. But God's love for us is so perfect and his hopes so high and his design so exquisite that any reckless spoiling of it on our part turns us into combatants.

But here is the truth of the war and the wonderful truth of the armistice: "Once you were alienated from God and were enemies in your minds because of your evil behavior. But now he has reconciled you by Christ's physical body through death to present you holy in his sight, without blemish and free from accusation" (Col. 1:21–22).

"He has reconciled you" means that God did what only God can do. Only humanity should solve the spiritual problem of sin and alienation and hostility, but only God could. And so God became man. God followed through on his promise long-voiced through the prophets of the Old Testament: "I will be their God and they will be my people." That was God's way of saying that reconciliation is the right thing and that he would make it happen.

Now, it wouldn't make much sense for God to provide a way of peace between himself and individual human beings but not a way for human beings to make peace between themselves. It may be true that this world will always have wars and that neighbors will always fight, but the peace that God brings between individuals and himself does bring chapters of reconciliation into the human story as well.

As ironic as it was in the 1800s for some people in the troubled United States to say, "We will be reconciled no matter how many of you we need to kill," it is nothing compared to the Savior saying, "We will be reconciled no matter how much of *my* blood will need to be spilled." The blood of the God-man—every pure, innocent, full-of-life drop—was the complete payment for a truly just peace, a peace that will last not just for a year, a decade, or a century but for eternity.

Pray This

God, I know that only peace with you will make my life right. I take it by faith that you have made that possible. I am in awe of what you chose to do in the sacrifice of the Lord Jesus on my behalf. Make gratitude the posture of my life, and let me bring peace to others.

For Reflection or Discussion

1. In what area of your life are you enjoying peace at this time? In what area do you need peace?
2. Why do we find it so difficult to recognize and cooperate with the divine order of things?
3. What are some mistaken ways of trying to reconcile ourselves with God?
4. When you think about Christ on the cross and the idea of being at peace with God because of that sacrifice, how does that motivate you?

CLEANING UP YOUR ACT

18

> Virtue is not the absence of vices or
> the avoidance of moral dangers;
> virtue is a vivid and separate thing,
> like pain or a particular smell.
> — G. K. Chesterton

A small group enters the Navajo hut, led by a cantor who walks around a blazing fire in the middle, leaping over its flames and walking close enough to get singed. The purification rite has begun. Chanting in four directions. Sweat begins to run. An audience enters, and the business at hand gets serious. The cantor takes wooden pokers that have been heated in the fire and applies them to his bare skin, mostly on his legs, and then to the skin of those seeking purification. A special solution is poured into bowls in front the participants, which they drink. Their bellies begin to convulse until they vomit into the bowls—an absolute requirement of the rite. As the group leaves the hut, they place the bowls in a line, leaving them to the elements. Back inside the hut, where the fire is stirred and sweat pours freely, the cantor ends by sprinkling everybody with a lotion and fumigating them with incense.

Almost every civilization seeks purification. How people seek it varies widely, but they seek the same end: to be rid of what pollutes us and to enjoy that elusive quality—purity.

In Bali, when a child is three months old, a ritual is performed to transfer the pollution of the child to a chicken, which is then kept as a pet so that it can continue to absorb impurities. Such chickens are never killed and are never eaten but are buried with dignity when they die. (Bad deal for chickens: live in some cultures and they eat you; live in another culture and they may use you as a depository for sin.)

Other groups have bloodletting rituals, and many have washing rituals. But before I cringe at how odd the rituals seem to me, I must stop and notice one remarkable thing: human beings almost universally are desperately looking for purification.

We All Need Cleansing

The consensus is loud and clear: the world is a dirty place, and we need cleansing. Even the people you can think of who seem to want to sink lower and lower, to live in the dirt and call it home—what do you think they think about in the quiet, alone moments? You've got to believe that most of them wonder, "Isn't there something better than this?"

Someone who had never heard of the Old Testament scapegoat, sent into the desert with the sin of the people symbolically placed on it, or who had never heard of Jesus dying on the cross as a sacrifice for the sins of the world, might think of these things as strikingly odd too. But they are not magical transactions. The Israelites understood that when the goat was released into the wilderness, this shouted out the truth that God our Creator wants our sins removed from us, as far away as the east is from the west. The goat did nothing. The rite had significance only because it signified the spiritual realities of who God is, what he wants, and how he works in our lives. No Israelite should have thought, "I'm a hateful person, I beat my wife, I steal and cheat; thank God all the guilt for that is now loping out across the desert and no longer has anything to do with me. Nobody expects me to change. After all, there will be another goat next year."

No, it's not about the rite. Similarly, marriage is a relationship, not a ring; being an heir is about progeny, not wills; and purification is about life change, not just spiritual sleight of hand.

At the heart of purification, from a biblical point of view, is the idea of holiness. As an action and a process, holiness is called *sanctification*.

WHAT DOES GOD WANT FROM ME?

What does God want of my life, and what does he want to do in my life? It's all there in a single word: "This is the will of God: your *sanctification*" (1 Thess. 4:7, my trans.). Purification is not our desperate attempt to get out of the mud and vomit the poison. It is a life mission, and the Creator is leading the effort. That's a good thing, because human beings are no more able to purify themselves than gold ore mined from a mountain can turn itself into crowns and rings.

The idea that we need someone else's help to do what seems to be our responsibility is hard for many people to accept. Living a "clean" life is our responsibility, and we can't pull it off on our own. Have you ever made a resolution to improve your life in some significant way and been disappointed to find that your resolve lasted about thirty days (or thirty minutes) and then you were back to your old ways? I'm not talking about something as simple as changing your eating habits or exercise routines. I'm talking about change of the heart. "I'm going to start being a patient person—right now!" "I'm going to decide not to have this hot anger inside that keeps burning other people." "I'm going to stop obsessing about the things I want and stop being jealous of others who have more than I do." I, I, I. It's like asking a man standing in a barrel how far off the ground he thinks he can lift himself.

The list could go on and on. Certainly there are people who would step forward and say, "I have made resolutions to change my basic attitude and to behave better around other people, and I think

I've improved, so don't tell me I need God's help." But that raises a couple of questions: Where, then, did you get the concept of how your life could be better? And where do you think you got the desire to clean up your act, if not from God? And how complete and enduring do you want your purification to be?

But the most important question is about the forward trajectory of our lives: What are we counting on to get us on the right track, keep us on the right track, and give us the spiritual energy to move down that track?

HOLINESS

Holiness means "distinctiveness or separateness." Over a thousand times in the Old Testament someone or something is called "holy." Usually it is God, who is utterly distinct—not in the sense of being removed, uninvolved, or indifferent—but in the sense of being pure. Other times the word is used of teaching devices in the Old Testament to drive home the point that amid the commonness of this world's pollution, some things can be different. A holy priesthood, holy rites, even a holy (consecrated) temple, altar, and temple furnishings.

To seek purification is to seek differentness. Things can be better than they are. Human beings can be better than they typically are. We can do better than the vulgar (a word whose root means "common"). Your experience in life can be higher and better than living like a breathing-eating-working machine with soft parts.

Now here is where that differentness begins: God's declaration. When the New Testament talks about those who are "saints" (literally, "holy ones"), it means all those who have a connection with God by believing in Christ. The apostle Paul begins many of his letters by addressing "the saints" in the churches he is writing to, by which he means all the believers, not just a separate, superholy class. Here is a simple but radical idea: because a believer belongs to God, he or she has been "set apart" by God even before he or she starts acting set apart or holy. You are a saint, in other words, even before you act like one. It is like a parent teaching a growing child through example to think bigger thoughts, use bigger words, and act on bigger principles. You teach a twelve-year-old a bigger vocabulary by using fifteen-year-old words.

I recently got a new car that my wife and I agreed would be set apart for my travels and my work. We have two teenagers in our household, and both are new drivers, so our vehicles are very heavily used, with plenty of dents and dings mysteriously appearing and lots of fast food wrappers that also mysteriously appear. So the plan is that Dad's new car will be set apart for a different use than hauling bags of manure from the garden store. The "set-apartness" was simply a declaration (and, to help the cause, not giving anybody else a key to the car).

That's the picture we get in the Bible of special priestly garments and temple furniture that were set apart, as were prophets, priests, and kings. All it takes is a declaration from God. He says, *that* table will be my altar, *that* man will be my prophet, *that* land will be a place of promise, *that* Abram will become Abraham. How did Abraham qualify to be the father of a nation and the picture of faith to the whole world? God chose, Abram believed, and so he was set apart.

Anyone who believes in Jesus Christ has been declared by God: "Holy!"

PURIFICATION: AN ONGOING PROCESS

The purification process never ends as long as we live on earth. Nobody will ever rightly hold their "holiness" over you, because all of us are enrolled in the same program. In fact, it is when people start to flaunt their personal holiness that you start to worry about them getting putrefied rather than purified. Even the great apostle Paul, summarizing his life, said, "*Not* that I have already obtained all this, or have already been made *perfect*, but I press on to take hold of that for which Christ Jesus took hold of me" (Phil. 3:12, italics mine).

Holiness is a past, present, and future reality. "You were washed, you were sanctified, you were justified in the name of the Lord Jesus Christ and by the Spirit of our God" (1 Cor. 6:11).

And it has precious little to do with sweat or vomiting.

May God himself, the God of peace, sanctify you through and through. May your whole spirit, soul and body be kept blameless at the coming of our Lord Jesus Christ. The one who calls you is faithful and he will do it.

—1 Thessalonians 5:23–24

Pray This

Dear God, purify me inside and out. Cleanse me and I will be clean. Cleanse my mind. Purify my heart. Suppress my motives that are self-centered and small. Help me believe what you mean when you call us saints.

For Reflection or Discussion

1. Why might a person sneer or look confused if someone were to say, "I want to be more holy"?
2. What areas of your life need purification right now?
3. If you are a believer, do you find it easy or difficult to believe that God has already set you apart?
4. What disappointments have you had in seeking improvements in your life?
5. How has God used other people, life circumstances, or his Word to do an act of cleansing in your life?

SANCTUARY

19

I believe in the communion of the saints.
—*The Apostles' Creed*

A survivor shuffles through the rubble of what used to be his home before a tornado pulled it apart into a hundred thousand pieces. What was shelter is now a pile of broken boards and bricks. The man stands beneath an empty sky where a roof used to cover his head. He stoops to pick up a bent and wet family photo. "We lost everything," he says. "Absolutely everything."

We've all seen that kind of picture on television news. The camera is always attracted to desolation. But what we don't see is the family in the weeks and months that follow, as they try to reframe their lives after it has all blown to pieces. We don't see what happens in a person's heart when that sanctuary disappears and the pieces fall apart.

LOSING YOUR SANCTUARY

It is hard for us to imagine what it must have been like for the Israelites when they returned to Jerusalem fifty years after it had been leveled by the Babylonians. Looking across the Kidron Valley, they saw rocks and boulders strewn about, some of them still black with soot from the fires their grandfathers had seen burning. Jerusalem lay silent, but in the sound of the wind, one might have imagined the shouts of men, women, and children on that terrible day when the Babylonian soldiers breached the wall. But worse than anything else was the communal memory of the great temple of Solomon being pulled apart wall by wall by teams of horses and ropes, looters scurrying away with the bronze and silver and gold they had stripped from the temple. It was not just a devastation that the people thought wouldn't happen; it was something that *couldn't* happen. Not the temple. Not if God was the kind of Lord he said he was.

What do you do when you've lost your sanctuary?

On the day of the Israelites' return to Jerusalem, a younger generation who had grown up in exile on the fertile plains of the Tigris and Euphrates looked at their ancestral home and contemplated their plans to rebuild it. It was time to take a graveyard of rubble and make a new beginning. Time to put the pieces back together. It would take courage to do so. The surrounding tribes would rather that Jerusalem remain a pile of stones than become a thriving community again. The enemies jeered. "Can they bring the stones back to life those heaps of rubble?" (Neh. 4:2). But God had given Ezra the priest and Nehemiah the governor the vision and faith to proceed. Their words built the people up, and the people built the city. Ezra, the spiritual leader of the project, put it this way: "[God] has granted us new life to rebuild the house of our God and repair its ruins" (Ezra 9:9).

Remarkably, the Israelites began with the heart of it. Before they had protective walls, before they had proper homes, they built an altar. Right there on the high plateau on the east side of the city, right out in the open and within plain view of their enemies, they built an altar as if to say, "There is only one place to begin again; we must meet God in worship."

MEETING GOD IN WORSHIP

I've met so many people over the years who can identify with the Israelites. Their sanctuary has been leveled, that place in their lives where they felt safe and secure. A spouse may have died, and even though everyone knows the rule going into marriage—"till death do us part"—the parting still seems like a devastating tornado. A person may have been fired from his or her job. A child died of leukemia. A relationship turned bitter. Life fell to pieces.

Many people who have lost their sanctuary will tell you that the only thing they could cling to was God. Amid unanswered questions and a threatening sky, an instinct inside said, "Run to God, and wedge yourself into him as if into the crevasse of a great mountain. Or, better yet, seek God at the temple."

No temple stands in Jerusalem today, and it is probably hard for us to imagine what a soul-satisfying sight the temple was to the Israelites. It was the fixed point of their lives, the center of the map, the sanctuary that reminded them of the safety of God, even if they lived miles away. The temple was a statement: God is here; he has a foothold in the world.

God is not contained in a temple. Rather, the temple was a statement that the great God who sits above the circle of the earth and who weighs nations like dust on a scale maintains contact with this world. He receives sacrifices and he gives oracles at the temple. The pillars speak of his strength, and the gold of his incomparable worth. The priesthood is evidence that mortals can stand before God (*priest* means "one who stands").

A NEW, LIVING COMMUNITY

But an invading army could and did knock down that temple in Jerusalem. More than six hundred years later, another army, the Romans, would break down the new temple building that Herod built a few decades after they struck down the temple that was Jesus' body. But one of Jesus' followers, a man whom Jesus called "Rock," wrote about a brand-new kind of temple. A new community of Jesus' followers was being built into a new kind of temple. In the first epistle of Peter we read: "You also, like living stones, are being built into a spiritual house to be a holy priesthood, offering spiritual sacrifices acceptable to God through Jesus Christ" (1 Peter 2:5).

What a remarkable thought! We always tend to think that our sanctuary—that safe, right place of life—is outside ourselves. It is our marriage, our home, our job, a friendship, a role. But Mr. Rock called *people* living stones and said they are the building blocks that God uses. Your life is designed to be brought together with other lives in a great construction project designed and managed by God himself.

The apostle Paul put it this way: "You are . . . fellow citizens with God's people and members of God's household, built on the foundation of the apostles and prophets, with Christ Jesus himself as the chief cornerstone. In him the whole building is joined together and rises to become a holy temple in the Lord. And in him you too are being built together to become a dwelling in which God lives by his Spirit" (Eph. 2:19–22).

This is the church. A sanctuary God is building by putting together the pieces of what human community should have been in the first place. Forget for a moment every idea of the church you've ever heard. Many of them we should try to forget permanently because we have so corrupted the meaning of the church and the church has so often fallen short of what God designed it to be. The church is supposed to be a living community built out of living stones, but we have often made it a dead, hollow place. Worse than that, when we hear the word *church* we think of that building on the corner of Brick Street and Board Street, repeating the errors of God's people in the Old Testament when they thought their temple's glory was in the stones and gold, rather than in people and God.

The church has failed so often and in so many ways, which was probably inevitable because it is built with the flawed material of humanity. We have traded the righteousness of God for our tinny self-righteousness. We've been satisfied with a club when it should be a community. We've used the church to build walls instead of open doors. We've sunk to intertribal warfare between churches instead of marveling at the one place in the world—really, the only place in the world—where we can see "every nation, tribe, people, and language" (Rev. 7:9) flourish together.

We have often thought of the church as a place to settle in, rather than as an army ready to march. Instead of serving as a community in which deep spiritual healing can occur, the church often has become a dangerous place where sharp edges and projectiles injure and wound. The church should lead the way as the high-water mark of intellectual inquiry, but we are often satisfied with blunt-edged simplicity. The church should prove itself as the most creative community in society, but we often think the blander the better.

GOD IS BUILDING

Yet God is building a church. No matter how hard we work against it, God is intent on staying with the original plan. Jesus said, "I will build my church." So who will argue? The apostle Paul, in the passage quoted above, said, "You *are* being built together." And Jesus is laid down as the chief cornerstone, the fixed reference point for every other stone that will be laid down.

I built a retaining wall in our backyard fifteen years ago, and I'm amazed to say it still stands. For all the flaws in the way I built that wall, I did follow one good piece of advice someone gave me before I ever started: make sure the first block is put in *exactly* the right place, perfectly level. I did that, spending an inordinate amount of time getting that one block laid. That cornerstone became the reference point, and the rest of the stones knew exactly where they needed to line up.

There is our hope. Jesus is the cornerstone, and God's own hand will take our rough-edged lives, which are the living stones, and skillfully put them together. And the church rises. It is not necessarily more impressive than other human organizations from a human point of view, but it rises above any other ambition any other architect has imagined. The purpose of the church is to be a community in which God dwells.

Skeptics and enemies will say, "Can they bring stones back to life from rubble?" Believing Christians themselves may wonder, "Is this thing really going to work?" But the wise person says, "If God states he's going to do something, who am I to doubt? I'd rather throw my life into something God intends to build than stand outside and debate whether it's possible or not."

When I think about all the lofty descriptions of the church in the New Testament and then go into my office day after day, I find myself continually comparing the reality to the principle. Is the church really that sanctuary, that spiritual house, that Peter and Paul talked about? Do people actually find healing and protection there? Is the church something we can be proud of, as the Israelites were proud of the spectacular temple Solomon built, from which the smoke of offerings wafted across the valley below?

The truth is we have good days and bad days—just as it was at the temple, just as it is in anyone's marriage. The temple was an ideal, but a lot of nonsense went on in its courtyards: proud priests, superstitious worshipers, money changers who thought of nothing but commercial activity. But despite the flaws, the ideal is not compromised, and God keeps doing mighty deeds through the fellowship of believers.

That's the way I must think about the church and the particular congregation where I worship and serve. Christ has called the church his bride. So who will dare step forward and insult Christ by saying that she'll never amount to anything? Dare anyone say, "Have you taken a really good look at her, Jesus? A groom knows what he's really gotten into only when he shuts the door behind him"?

So I regularly remind the people in our church that we are a flawed community. A community in which, at some point, you will probably be disappointed or misunderstood or unappreciated. But unless the church looks honestly at what it is and what it isn't, unless it can state and hold to reality, what good is it to say that the church is a place to find the truth?

Then I look at the many people who come to worship who are wise enough to know that the church is not the issue of the day. They are there to find God. They hope to hear a word from God. They are willing to hear words that challenge or convict as well as words that comfort and cheer. They want to raise their own voices in praise and to do it, not in the isolation of their own home or car but in the sanctuary, with a people. They are glad to see people who are twenty years younger than them and twenty years older than them sitting nearby. They want to know who has just had a tornado come through their lives so that they can help and extend mercy. And they are glad for those who are doing quite well at the moment, because the church is a place where strength and weakness are always balancing each other.

The church is like no other place on earth.

Pray This

Lord, help me to find you in the sanctuaries you have provided. I know that there is no group of human beings that will not have flaws. But help me to find my place in your new community, the church. Help me to behave like a bride deeply loved by a perfect husband. Restore us where our walls have fallen. Correct us when we have gotten diverted from our mission and message.

For Reflection or Discussion

1. What disappointments about the church stand in the way of your belief in its purposes?
2. Where have you seen God's new community as a place where he dwells and works?
3. In what ways is Jesus the reference point for the building of the church?
4. What do you bring to the church in terms of needs and resources?

THE CLASH
OF KINGDOMS

20

I will place no value on anything
I have or may possess except in relation
to the kingdom of Christ.
— *David Livingstone*

In the weeks leading up to the beginning of the
war with Iraq in 2003, I found that many
people were tracking the unfolding international
crisis with rapt attention. On the other hand, I
said to the young woman cutting my hair one
day, "You have of a lot of conversations with
people sitting in this chair. What are they saying
about the international crisis?" She said (and I
can't say I was surprised), "Nothing at all. People
aren't saying anything."

Perhaps that's because we often didn't know
what to say, and many people didn't know what
to think. Others knew exactly what they thought,
and many of them had a fairly simple approach:
"War is an evil, and so it should be rejected,
period." Others thought, "You see evil over
there, you've got a big stick in your hand, so
you know what you should do." But life isn't as
simple as either of these options. It's a complicated world, and it's getting more complicated
all the time. How has the world changed since

September 11? How have the rules changed in the world because of weapons of mass destruction?

Recent events raise many questions about living in an earthly kingdom and in the kingdom of God at the same time. What does it mean to be a Christian citizen? If you believe that you live within and under the kingdom of Christ but that you also hold citizenship in the country in which you live, how do these two realities work together?

What do you do when those kingdoms seem to clash?

In his epistle to the Romans, the apostle Paul lays out a bold set of principles:

> Everyone must submit himself to the governing authorities, for there is no authority except that which God has established. The authorities that exist have been established by God. Consequently, he who rebels against the authority is rebelling against what God has instituted, and those who do so will bring judgment on themselves. For rulers hold no terror for those who do right, but for those who do wrong. Do you want to be free from fear of the one in authority? Then do what is right and he will commend you. For he is God's servant to do you good. But if you do wrong, be afraid, for he does not bear the sword for nothing. He is God's servant, an agent of wrath to bring punishment on the wrongdoer. Therefore, it is necessary to submit to the authorities, not only because of possible punishment but also because of conscience.
>
> This is also why you pay taxes, for the authorities are God's servants, who give their full time to governing. Give everyone what you owe him: If you owe taxes, pay taxes; if revenue, then revenue; if respect, then respect; if honor, then honor.
>
> —ROMANS 13:1–7

The clash of kingdoms sometimes turns to war between earthly nations. But there is also a wide and deep teaching in Scripture about the kingdom of God and how it relates to the kingdoms of this world, the nations. Sometimes these kingdoms clash; sometimes they don't.

One truth at the center of Jesus' teaching, at the very core of his message, was that the kingdom of God had come. Jesus himself said, "I must preach the good news of the kingdom of God . . . because that is why I was sent" (Luke 4:43). The Old Testament, particularly the prophetic books, clearly teaches that a future day would come when the kingdom of God would usher in a new age. The Old Testament divides cosmic history into two parts: this age and the age to come. In this age, God's people are to do their best to live through the periods of peace and the periods of conflict and war that are the everyday realities of this world. But there will come a time when God will impose upon the world his power and his ruling and usher in the age to come.

In Jesus' day, people still looked forward to the age to come. And today we are still looking forward to the day of the Lord, when history will draw to a close and God will remake everything. But Jesus dramatically adapted this view of reality. He taught that though the age to come is still to come, the kingdom of God had already come.

If you are a believer in Jesus here and now, whether your home country is the United States or Syria or Israel, Argentina or Ireland or Iran, the most important reality of your life is that you live within and under the kingdom of Christ.

BELONGING TO THE KINGDOM OF GOD

Belonging to the kingdom of God means a number of life-changing realities. It means a life elevated by the awareness of a higher kingdom that inspires higher aspirations.

WE KNOW THE KINGDOM HAS COME

First, belonging to the kingdom of Christ means we know the kingdom has come. In Matthew 12:28, Jesus said, "If I drive out demons by the Spirit of God, then the kingdom of God has come upon you." He said similar things when he healed people and showed his authority. That is the whole point of the miraculous earthly ministry of Jesus. He was proving that God had come into the world in a new and powerful way. Satan would be bound like a dog on a short leash. Death would no longer have the power of fear in human hearts. Because the King had come, his kingdom had come. In Luke 17:20–21, the Pharisees asked Jesus when the kingdom of God would come.

Jesus replied, "The kingdom of God does not come with your careful observation, nor will people say, 'Here it is,' or 'There it is,' because the kingdom of God is within [or among] you." This was a radical statement. When everybody looked forward to the day when God would fix everything, set up his kingdom in a specific nation, and sort out the good guys and the bad guys once and for all, Jesus said, "Take a look, and you will see that God's reigning power is right here among you, because I am among you."

WE HAVE A DIFFERENT SOURCE OF LIFE

Second, belonging to the kingdom of Christ means we have a different source of life. Jesus said, "No one can enter the kingdom of God unless he is born of water and the Spirit. . . . You must be born again." Living in the kingdom of Christ means we have a different way of life because we have a different source of life. Spiritual birth means our hearts long for what God loves, our emotions respond to things that are good and right, and our minds are awakened to what God is doing and are sharpened by the specific teachings that come through his Word. We're alive to God and alive to the world around us. When we see kingdoms in conflict, our hearts break because we know that if everybody were born into and lived under the goodness and authority of the kingdom of Christ, life would be different.

WE TAKE A HUMBLE POSITION

Third, belonging to the kingdom of Christ means we take a humble position in life. In Matthew 18:3–4, with a little child standing between him and his disciples, Jesus said, "I tell you the truth, unless you change and become like little children, you will never enter the kingdom of heaven. Therefore, whoever humbles himself like this child is the greatest in the kingdom of heaven." The kingdom of Christ, in other words, demands that we act with humility instead of arrogance, that we trust in God's power more than in our own power. It is a very different way of living. It is unlike anything we see anywhere else in the world. The more we have, the more we can serve. To whom much has been given, much is expected.

We Seek the Kingdom of Christ, We Don't Create It

Fourth, belonging to the kingdom of Christ means we seek the kingdom; we don't create it. In the Sermon on the Mount, Jesus said, "Seek first his kingdom and his righteousness, and all these things will be given to you as well." We don't build God's kingdom. God's kingdom exists *because* he reigns, not as an institution or church or nation *in which* he reigns. So we seek it. We submit to it. And God does what only God can do, and it is more immensely powerful in changing the world than any other power at work.

We Value Heavenly Citizenship above All Else

Fifth, belonging to the kingdom of Christ means we value our heavenly citizenship more than anything else. That's why Jesus said in Matthew 13 that the kingdom of heaven is like treasure hidden in a field. It is like finding a pearl of immense value and giving up everything you have so that you can own that pearl. I ask myself, "Is my citizenship in the kingdom of Christ the most valuable thing in my life? Is it worth more to me than all that I possess, more than all the people in my life, more than anything else I am aspiring to in life?"

Parents can do nothing better for their children than to make coming under Christ as their personal ruler the most important and daily priority of their lives. Kids can do nothing more important for their future than to come under the reigning power of Christ's kingdom—and to stay there for a lifetime, no matter where they live, no matter what they do.

Belonging to the kingdom of Christ also means seeing the power of the small and the hidden. In Matthew 13, Jesus also said the kingdom of God is like good seed planted in soil, a tiny mustard seed that grows into the largest of the garden plants, and the invisible yeast in a loaf of bread that transforms it. That's why the small and almost hidden ministry of Jesus among a handful of people was an event that spread through the whole world and changed the world. Nothing like it has ever happened in the history of the world. The apostle Paul was a poor public speaker who didn't have a strong personal presence, but he carried the fire of the gospel of Christ and lit the world on fire with it. What does the church have to offer in a world in which the big news is the continual conflict of kingdoms? The church offers the message that Christ can rule, beginning in the heart. That message is like a tiny seed or a pinch of yeast that can cross borders and can root itself where earthly rulers want it eliminated, and it will grow.

WE HAVE A MESSAGE TO PROCLAIM

Finally, belonging to the kingdom of Christ means we have a message to proclaim. It was Jesus' message, and it was the message he entrusted to his followers. Jesus sent his disciples out to go from town to town and said, "Go, preach this message: 'The kingdom of heaven is near'" (Matt. 10:7). Jesus also told his followers, "Nation will rise against nation, and kingdom against kingdom. There will be famines and earthquakes in various places. . . . And this gospel of the kingdom will be preached in the whole world as a testimony to all nations, and then the end will come" (Matt. 24:7, 14).

Bearing the message that Christ wants every person to submit to his reigning power is the one thing holding the church together in Africa and Asia and the Middle East and South America. British Christians believe it; so do Chinese Christians and Argentinian Christians. The kingdom of Christ has come, and the world will never be the same.

This is what it means to belong to the kingdom of Christ.

BELONGING TO AN EARTHLY KINGDOM

If you stopped there, you might think that because Christians live under the domain of Christ's kingdom, they can be oblivious to the earthly kingdom in which they live, or act indifferently, or even antagonistically, toward it. But God's Word does not teach that we are to act indifferently toward the communities and nations we live in. Nor does it teach that Christ's kingdom becomes incarnate in any earthly kingdom, which was disappointing news to Jesus' listeners. These earthly kingdoms, which are of a very different nature than the kingdom of Christ, are also part of God's way of offering law and order in this disorderly world. That is the essential meaning of Romans 13. So let's look there, point by point.

We Welcome Order

The first principle in Romans 13 is that belonging to an earthly kingdom means we accept God-established authority in government, which is the providential way order can come to societies. Paul tells us that "the authorities that exist have been established by God" (v. 1). It is remarkable that Paul would say this, given the fact that there always have been and always will be many lousy governments in the world, including the Roman Empire in which Paul lived and was a citizen. It was an efficient government, but it was also arbitrary, aggressive, and sometimes cruel. Emperor Nero was a madman who martyred many Christians, tossing them to wild beasts or covering their bodies in tar and lighting them as human torches in the arena. Yet living in anarchy is not a better alternative. Try living in a place where there is no government at all, a place like Somalia, for instance, and you will realize that even a deeply flawed government is usually better than no government at all.

We Look for Justice from Earthly Authority

Second, belonging to an earthly kingdom means we look for justice from that earthly authority. The way things are supposed to work is for rulers to hold sanctions against those who do wrong, and that is a part of the ordering of a sinful and out-of-control world. It is one of the basic, God-given functions of government.

But what if that all gets turned upside down? What if the earthly authority produces terror not for those who do wrong but for those who do right? Is there a time when an earthly authority has so violated justice, so misused power, that it should be resisted and even overthrown? That has been the rationale behind "just war."

We Expect That Earthly Authority Will Wield the Sword

Third, belonging to an earthly kingdom means we expect that the earthly authority will wield the sword, that is, sanctions and punishment (v. 4). Here Paul tells us that one of the most terrible responsibilities of an earthly kingdom, the responsibility to apply punishment and sanctions, is part of the ordering of societies. Because of sin and crime and injustice and evil, the sad reality is that the sword still needs to be used, but it should be used only in the cause of order and justice.

We Pay Our Dues to Society

Fourth, belonging to an earthly kingdom means we pay our dues to society. One of the least quoted verses in the Bible is Romans 13:6–7: "This is also why you pay taxes.... If you owe taxes, pay taxes." Very few people have underlined those words in their Bibles. If we want to receive the benefits of living in the order of governed society, we have to pay our dues for that privilege—because fire engines and roads and schools and even swords don't come free. A good citizen asks not only, "What benefits can come my way from my country?" but also, "What are my obligations to support my society?"

We Are Committed to Social Realism and Responsibility

Finally, belonging to an earthly kingdom means we are committed to social realism and social responsibility. Verse 7 says to give respect where respect is due and honor where honor is due.

Living in Two Kingdoms

To sum up, Scripture teaches that God's order comes to us directly in the kingdom of Christ, which broke into the world when Christ came. God's dynamic reign in our lives happens no matter where we are, no matter how old we are, no matter whether we're strong or weak, rich or poor. It is a kingdom that works in hidden ways and secret ways. It is a relationship with God that begins with being born from above and is lived out with the attitude of a trusting child. It transforms your life. It banishes fear of death. It gives us purpose and meaning in life and a message to proclaim.

But God also works in the world through earthly kingdoms. We need societies with rules. We need governing. We need law and order. Sometimes we need swords. We will always have to pay taxes. And so the Christian prays, "Thy kingdom come, thy will be done on earth as it is in heaven."

Now, there's the rub. How are we to live in two kingdoms at once? That is a question Christians have been wrestling with since the earliest days.

Living in two kingdoms means, first of all, that we're not surprised when nation rises against nation. Jesus said that is exactly what we should expect. He said, "Nation will rise against nation, and kingdom against kingdom." Kingdoms will continue to clash. It is what we all have to deal with here at the beginning of the twenty-first century—only now the nations have weapons that no one could have conceived of years ago.

If you believe that God works in two different kinds of kingdoms—the kingdom of Christ and the kingdoms of this world—you have to acknowledge that sometimes the sword is needed, but you also have to believe, because Jesus taught that "Blessed are the peacemakers," that war is a last resort and a tragic outcome even in a just cause. You have to believe that nations will never fully eradicate evil through political or military action, and so we should not expect it. You have to believe that there is a difference between just war and unjust war, a distinction Christians have been trying to define for the past sixteen hundred years. Some of the central criteria for just war will always include self-defense and the protection of innocent people, even with the rapidly changing technology of war and the insidious nature of terrorism. You also have to believe that international diplomacy is worth the effort no matter how messy, because, as Romans 13 teaches, God works in and through nations in the interest of order, however imperfect we are.

To belong to two kingdoms at once means we live in tension; we must never confuse the two. In Matthew 13:11, Jesus said, "The knowledge of the secrets of the kingdom of heaven has been given to you." That a person can live in America, or Germany, or Brazil, or France, or Korea, and still believe that he or she belongs to a higher kingdom is a mystery, and even a secret, that much of the world cannot understand. The communist government in China, which kicked

Christian missionaries out in the 1940s and tried to eradicate Christianity as recently as the 1960s, had no idea of the mystery of a kingdom in people's hearts that would cause Chinese believers to grow from thousands to hundreds of thousands to millions to tens of millions. It is a mystery because most people don't believe that the God and the Maker of the universe actually reigns in the world today. A secular view says that the things that motivate people are money, ideologies, and national interest. But the mystery of the kingdom of God is that if Christ rules in your heart, he compels you to be a law-abiding citizen, a moral person, a selfless person. He makes you a law-abiding citizen because you want what is good, not just for yourself but for others who live in your community. This is where the kingdoms converge. We know Scripture commands us to pray for our political leaders, and we can pray in particular for those political leaders who display a genuine faith in Christ, that they would be strengthened and given wisdom from the kingdom of Christ in the service of the earthly kingdoms they influence.

Any leader in any earthly society must wonder how in the world to hold that society together. In communities, as in physical bodies, things will fall to pieces unless something holds them together. Laws can constrain, and a sense of duty may result in self-sacrifice for the higher good, but the best hope any earthly kingdom has is if the citizenry has a sense of conscience that pulls the pieces together.

Christ reigning in our hearts should motivate us to civic responsibility that goes well beyond what any kingdom with the best of rules and laws can define. In China, I sat at a table where communist officials and church leaders talked about how Christians distinguish themselves in their communities as the one group that genuinely looks out for the welfare of the community. What's the secret? What's the mystery? It is to live in the awareness that you are in two kingdoms at once and to believe that God can work in both.

Belonging to two kingdoms means that we know that the kingdom of the world will one day become the kingdom of Christ. That's exactly what it says in Revelation 11:15: "The seventh angel sounded his trumpet, and there were loud voices in heaven, which said: 'The kingdom of the world has become the kingdom of our Lord and of his Christ, and he will reign for ever and ever.'" Now, that will only happen when the day of the Lord comes and God draws all of history to a close.

On the day Jesus was crucified, two criminals were crucified beside him. The Roman sword with blunted judgment came against one innocent man as well as two guilty men. The two criminals, like the rest of us sinners, symbolize two kinds of choices. One looked at Jesus as a miserable excuse for a leader. A ruler who had no rule. A political wannabe who had no following. A king who had no kingdom. A joke. And he rejected him.

The other criminal looked at Jesus and said the most important words a human being can say: "Remember me when you come into your kingdom." And he had no way of knowing how close he was. For the kingdom *had* come, and the King of Kings was right there. And so Jesus said to him, "Today . . . paradise."

PRAY THIS

Your kingdom come, your will be done, on earth as it is in heaven.

FOR REFLECTION OR DISCUSSION

1. In what ways have you seen the invisible kingdom of God at work?

2. What are your thoughts and feelings about the country you live in?

3. What would be a scenario in which your allegiance to one kingdom might contradict your allegiance to the other? What would you do?

4. In what ways do you see God bringing order through the earthly kingdom you are living in?

WHAT HAPPENS WHEN WE DIE?

21

The dread of something after death,
The undiscovered country from whose
    bourn [boundary]
No traveler returns.
—*William Shakespeare*, Hamlet

Two caskets were placed in the front of the church sanctuary and then surrounded with a sea of floral bouquets that had come from all over the country. Then family pictures, more beautifully striking than the flowers, were carefully positioned around the caskets. Husband and wife, each just forty-nine years old. Many friends and extended family members from the small town where they had lived most of their lives lined up to look into their faces.

Warren and Donna had been farmers for many years, until they sensed a call from God to become missionaries and to go help people in Africa in whatever way they could. Their last assignment in Uganda had them helping students learn how to make something of the crusty, thin soil in that place. But one terrible night, men in militia uniforms came to the couple's outpost, started the roof of their home on fire, and then shot them point-blank as they exited their home.

I had just stepped off an airplane and turned my cell phone on when it started to beep with a text message from my wife back home: "Sad news about missionaries. Call."

Thousands of people attended the couple's funeral. As a church, we had no idea that just several weeks later thousands of people would attend another funeral at our church, this time for a twenty-year-old woman, a National Guard reservist called to active duty in Iraq, who was shot as she defended her Humvee when it had come under fire. She was one of three sisters serving together in Iraq, two of them twins, each of them beautiful young women. Her death was a national news story.

When we gather at memorial services, people generally think about two things: How should I respond to this death and to the loved ones left grieving? And (whether we admit we ask this question or not) what do I really know about this doorway called death?

A QUESTION WE CAN'T HELP BUT ASK

What happens when we die?

This is a question we'd rather not ask, but it is so central to our experience and our destiny that we can't help but ask it. No one should be surprised that most people have at least some fear about death, because we naturally fear the unknown. Death is a door we look at our whole lives yet is closed to us our whole lives, until that one final instant when we cross the threshold. In Psalm 23, the portion of the Bible most often read at funerals, David wrote, "Though I walk through the valley of the shadow of death, I will fear no evil." Why? Because God is the Shepherd who cares. As David wrote, "Your rod and your staff, they comfort me. Surely goodness and mercy will follow me all the days of my life and I will dwell in the house of the Lord forever."

I visited Shirley in the hospice where she spent her final days. She was, toward the end, just lingering. She had barely enough strength to raise her head. She forced words up and out of her throat, but they were brilliant words, words that I've heard from many other people approaching the threshold: "I'm ready. I'm at peace. I know this is okay." It was very much as if Shirley was standing in one place with a shadow gradually coming over her, but she herself did not become darkness because her faith connection with God would not allow it. That is the key: passing through the valley, and even under the shadow, but knowing that God is right there, even having a stronger sense of him than when we were strong and virile.

I hardly ever think about my breathing, unless I'm sick and raspy. I don't think very often about my last breath, although I know that will come someday. Sometimes, as a pastor, I'm with people right at the end of their lives. One week I was with two very different people at their last breath.

Joe had been around the sun seventy-five times, had seen wars come and go, had lived on two continents. Olivia was born three months too early and saw only six days in her short life.

Joe looked like a typical grandpa. Bald on top, eyes enlarged by the lenses of his glasses, stooped and easily cold, he was the kind of patient the nurses loved to care for. Though a major stroke had slowed his body and mind, his face still responded to a kind word.

Joe's final days were not really his hardest. In the vitality of his youth, he had seen the world around him rise up in war. He lived in the Slavic area of central Europe. At the end of the war, the Communists came in to establish the new state of Yugoslavia. One day Joe owned his own home in his own village; the next he was a dispossessed refugee heading for Austria. Several years later he took his young wife and his eleven-year-old daughter to live in America.

In his latter days, Joe reverted to speaking the Old German he had learned as a boy. During the two months he spent at the hospital, the nurses got used to nodding with a smile as he mumbled words incomprehensible to their ears.

When he developed difficulty with his breathing, Joe's family knew that the end was near. A loving vigil started. First the grandchildren came to say good-bye through their tears; then his wife and daughter took over. For three days he was surrounded by soft words, warm blankets, strokes on the forehead. We read Psalm 23 aloud to him in German.

Joe's life developed a certain rhythm: drifting off to sleep, stopping breathing, waking in agitation, catching his breath, drifting off to sleep again—on and on. Occasionally he stopped breathing for a minute or more, which caused anyone in the room to stop breathing themselves until the sheets covering his chest slowly rose one more time.

I thought of the words of the gospel: "Jesus called out with a loud voice, 'Father, into your hands I commit my spirit.' When he had said this, he breathed his last." I knew that in both Hebrew and Greek the same word is used for *breath* and *spirit*. Breath is, after all, the most conspicuous vital sign. Breath often seems to us an ordinary thing, just an involuntary act. But to God, it is much more; breath was his voluntary gift to human beings who without him would merely be dirt. "The LORD God formed the man from the dust of the ground and breathed into his nostrils the breath of life, and the man became a living being." Paul said God himself "gives all people life and breath and everything else." How could it be any other way? God is the Breath that "moved across the waters" before he formed a world teeming with life; he is the Wind that "blows wherever it pleases."

Why did Job speak so often of breath? Was it that from his sickbed, he too felt his spirit slipping away? "Remember, O God, that my life is but a breath" (7:7). "In [God's] hand is the life of every creature and the breath of all mankind" (12:10). "As long as I have life within me, the breath of God in my nostrils, my lips will not speak wickedness" (27:3–4). "But it is the spirit in a man, the breath of the Almighty, that gives him understanding"(32:8). "The Spirit of God has made me; the breath of the Almighty gives me life" (33:4). "If it were his intention and he withdrew his spirit and breath, all mankind would perish together and man would return to the dust" (34:14).

"It's okay to rest, Joe," family and friends kept telling him, because they all knew that it really was okay. He was a man who looked like he was ready, really ready, to breathe his last, to let his spirit be committed to the God who created it. In the end, Joe's peace came quietly.

The weekend after Joe's death, I got a frightened call from Mary, a young mother and longtime friend whose second child, not due to be born for another three months, suddenly came into the world, frail and breathless. Olivia weighed one pound nine ounces when she was born and had time enough for only one small cry before the doctors and nurses whisked her away. Mother and daughter were separated for one long day, each in a different hospital. It was a great relief when Mary was able to join her husband, Marc, at the side of Olivia's Plexiglas home and could stroke her daughter through the armholes in the side of the incubator. They talked quietly to her; they taped a photo of themselves and her eighteen-month-old sister on the inside of the Plexiglas; they helped wash her and change her diapers, which were cut down to fit her minuscule frame.

She looked so pitifully fragile. Tubes attached to her arms, which were stretched out to her sides in cruciform shape. The plastic respirator tube was her only hope for life. Days two and three were encouraging; her color was good, her organs functioning well. Hope rose.

On the fourth day came the first ominous signs that her frail tissues were not faring well—hemorrhaging in the lungs, then in the brain, then in other organs. She did not look well, and the instruments around her looked more and more alien. A couple of days later, more bad news came: the damage was too severe; she would not make it.

The doctor explained that Marc and Mary could hold Olivia at the end if they wished, and they responded gratefully. It was a hushed time as Mary helped clean her baby one last time in the incubator, and when Olivia was brought to them in a quiet room, wrapped in a real baby blanket, she looked more comfortable than she ever had before. She was welcomed with tears and gentle whispers. She settled in as babies do when resting deeply, rocked back and forth, sung to gently.

The doctor had said that Olivia might continue to breathe for about five minutes after being taken off the respirator, but it turned out to be three and a half hours before the shallowest of breaths finally tapered off. There was no clear dividing line between life and death. Spirit parted from body as easily as the slow exhaling of an invisible and silent breath, and father and mother committed her to the Father.

What actually does happen when we die? The apostle Paul wrote of this in 2 Corinthians 5, when he was expecting that the persecuting authorities might kill him any day. Paul, skilled in the trade of tentmaking, compares our fragile, temporary bodies to tents. The tent will collapse some day, but the life goes on until it is joined to a resurrection body, a "heavenly dwelling," a home in heaven.

> For we know that when this earthly tent we live in is taken down—when we die and leave these bodies—we will have a home in heaven, an eternal body made for us by God himself and not by human hands. We grow weary in our present bodies, and we long for the day when we will put on our heavenly bodies like new clothing. For we will not be spirits without bodies, but we will put on new heavenly bodies. Our dying bodies make us groan and sigh, but it's not that we want to die and have no bodies at all. We want to slip into our new bodies so that these dying bodies will be swallowed up by everlasting life. God himself has prepared us for this, and as a guarantee he has given us his Holy Spirit.
>
> So we are always confident, even though we know that as long as we live in these bodies we are not at home with the Lord. That is why we live by believing and not by seeing. Yes, we are fully confident, and we would rather be away from these bodies, for then we will be at home with the Lord. So our aim is to please him always, whether we are here in this body or away from this body. For we must all stand before Christ to be judged. We will each receive whatever we deserve for the good or evil we have done in our bodies.
>
> —2 Corinthians 5:1–10 NLT

There are several important points in this passage.

1. Our present life is lived in a physical body, which, though a creation of God, is but a dwelling place, a tent.

2. Life after death includes some kind of resurrection body, which implies ongoing personal and conscious existence. As our earthly bodies are appropriate for life on earth, our heavenly bodies are suited for heaven (more on the meaning of *heaven* in the next chapter).

3. Leaving the bodies we have now makes it possible to be at home with the Lord (remember Jesus' words to the thief on the cross: "Today you will be with me in paradise").

4. Going through death is not a bad thing, because it means coming into the wonderful presence of God, a state beyond imagining.

5. It appears as though there is a kind of "intermediate state" between life in this body and life in the resurrection body, but that state includes the conscious knowledge of being in the presence and realm of God.

So even after death, after the body begins to fall apart in decay, God continues his ongoing constructive work, putting the pieces together. Just as our lives begin with God knitting us together in our mothers' wombs, for the end of life there is a mysterious preparation too. Death is not destruction but divine reconstruction in the resurrection.

Pray This

Lord, please help me not to fear that valley that I know I will have to approach, as does everyone else. Help me to know that the knowledge of your presence can grow stronger with each step we take toward you. Help me to trust you, and help me to be able to say with confidence, "Surely goodness and mercy will follow me, and I will dwell in the house of the Lord forever."

FOR REFLECTION OR DISCUSSION

1. How open do you think you are to considering the doorway of death?
2. What kinds of fears arise in us when we contemplate crossing the threshold of this life?
3. Can you think of someone who went to their end in this life with faith and hope? What did you notice about him or her?
4. How would you complete this sentence: "Lord, what I need from you when I see the shadow of that valley is . . ."?

THE NEW HEAVEN AND EARTH

22

Then I saw a new heaven
and a new earth,
for the first heaven and
the first earth had passed away.
—*Revelation 21:1*

The popular conception of heaven is something I don't want to have anything to do with.

Close your eyes. Picture heaven. What do you see, or not see? Are the images based on stories or movies, or on what Scripture actually says?

Whoever thought it was a good idea to depict heaven as the complete negation of everything good that we know in this life should be made to stand waist-deep in a cloud for ten years to see how he likes it.

This is a picture of a colorless heaven: white robes, white clouds, white everything. A heaven with no style. (Same old robes for millennia on end?) And the music? Now, I like harp music, for a while. An hour or two is just fine. But heaven can't possibly be harp music in a non-landscape, a mere cloud, with no activity and few conversations.

In attempts to depict a realm that is otherworldly, people have drifted toward images that are only subworldly. Even if we don't take these images literally, should we even suggest that the afterlife is basically the complete loss of everything good and beautiful we have experienced on earth?

The Bible speaks of fulfillment in heaven, something that makes life in this world seem only a shadow compared to the real thing. Heaven must be a life of continual discovery, of unceasing awe, where blue is bluer than you've ever seen it and fellowship with other people is like being in the best family in the world—nothing awry, nothing missing, nothing in excess. Heaven is a place of no tears because there is no reason for crying.

Peter put it this way: "But in keeping with his promise we are looking forward to a new heaven and a new earth, the home of righteousness" (2 Peter 3:13). Now, what precedes this is a fiery rebirth, but we'll come back to that.

Creation Groans for the Pieces to Be Put Back Together

I couldn't even guess how many times over the years I've talked with people about the losses and pains and disappointments of their lives in this world. They talk about their lives "falling apart" or "falling to pieces." And I've found that I come back to one Bible passage more than any other when I think of offering some assurance. It is a kind of map of all of life, and within its edges are the promises of life beyond this life. But mostly I turn to it because it so accurately captures the truth that though this world is bound to corruption, God and his undying love are the stable core of life, and out of that love, God is one day going to remake this world and remake us. Then there will be no more tears.

> I consider that our present sufferings are not worth comparing with the glory that will be revealed in us. The creation waits in eager expectation for the sons of God to be revealed. For the creation was subjected to frustration, not by its own choice, but by the will of the one who subjected it, in hope that the creation itself will be liberated from its bondage to decay and brought into the glorious freedom of the children of God.

We know that the whole creation has been groaning as in the pains of childbirth right up to the present time. Not only so, but we ourselves, who have the firstfruits of the Spirit, groan inwardly as we wait eagerly for our adoption as sons, the redemption of our bodies. For in this hope we were saved. But hope that is seen is no hope at all. Who hopes for what he already has? But if we hope for what we do not yet have, we wait for it patiently.

—ROMANS 8:18–25

A suffering man wrote these verses, and he truly believed that a future glory was ahead that would make our sufferings in this world close up like a wound that doesn't even leave a scar. Here is the honest assessment: the *whole* creation is frustrated by its bondage to decay. It is not just that human beings get divorced and get fired and get sick. Every living thing succumbs to decay. Every bird drops from the sky, and every tree falls. Earthquakes crack the world. Drought burns the land. There is a certain unfortunate consistency here, so we are not to think that when we go through a hard time, God is singling us out for special treatment. Yes, there may be a causal link in some forms of judgment, as when people put harmful drugs in their bodies or expose themselves to disease through sexual immorality. But many of our losses are not directly linked to particular mistakes and transgressions. We live in a diseased world. That may not be good news, but it is honest news, and it is the one explanation of life that is most consistently true.

And so "we groan inwardly as we eagerly await our adoption." Oh, God. Oh, God. How long? It is a groaning that is an expression not just of pain but of longing. That is why we say of a woman bearing a child that she is in labor, rather than that she is being tortured. It is pain toward an end, a spectacular end. And so the rest of creation joins with us in the groaning.

But there is "eager expectation" here, and real hope.

GOD'S LOVE IS RELENTLESS

Paul goes on to say (and notice how future and present, pain and restoration, are all reconciled):

And we know that in all things God works for the good of those who love him, who have been called according to his purpose. For those God foreknew he also predestined to be conformed to the likeness of his Son, that he might be the firstborn among many brothers. And those he predestined, he also called; those he called, he also justified; those he justified, he also glorified.

What, then, shall we say in response to this? If God if for us, who can be against us? He who did not spare his own Son, but gave him up for us all—how will he not also, along with him, graciously give us all things? Who will bring any charge against those whom God has chosen? It is God who justifies. Who is he that condemns? Christ Jesus, who died—more than that, who was raised to life—is at the right hand of God and is also interceding for us. Who shall separate us from the love of Christ? Shall trouble or hardship or persecution or famine or nakedness or danger or sword? . . .

No, in all these things we are more than conquerors through him who loved us. For I am convinced that neither death nor life, neither angels nor demons, neither the present nor the future, nor any powers, neither height nor depth, nor anything else in all creation, will be able to separate us from the love of God that is in Christ Jesus our Lord.

—Romans 8:28–35, 37–39

As many times as I've read this text, it still becomes more powerful each time I come back to it. For all of our piecemeal approaches to life, here is a singular perspective that brings together God and humanity, sin and forgiveness, suffering and health, death and life, loss and love.

God knows this world is broken. But he doesn't intend to leave it that way. We are in labor pains, but labor comes to an end, and then there is new life. Mighty forces work to separate us from God, but God's love is a bond that nothing can break. Something glorious is coming, and the substance of that glory is shining back into this day in which we live as surely as the glory of the first creation shines forward. We may feel as if we're stumbling in a cave, but light and life are all around us.

In the Old Testament, the prophets talked about the coming "day of the Lord." They spoke of two characteristics of that divine interruption of human affairs: judgment and vindication. God will settle scores. He will judge the wicked and vindicate their victims. A new kingdom is coming.

In the New Testament, the climax of human history unfolds in much greater detail. With the coming of Jesus, the Messiah, the kingdom of God has already been impressed upon this world. It is not a kingdom that can be located "here" or "there" but is, as Jesus said, "among you." Whenever Jesus healed someone, or cast out a demon, or performed some other miraculous sign, he was giving evidence that God's power was being unleashed in the world, although the remaking of the world will happen at a later time. He healed some people, but not all. Someone has compared our situation to D-day, when allied forces landed decisively on the coast of France and thereby signaled that the beginning of the end had come. But the end of the end only came years later, on V-day, victory day.

So we live in a kind of in-between time. D-day has happened, but V-day is yet to come. The kingdom of God has come, but the remaking of heaven and earth, the final redemption, is yet to come. Jesus has come, but one day he will return, a promise he made again and again in his teaching. He taught his followers that they should not speculate exactly when or how or where it will happen. But he also taught that his return was certain and that he would usher in both judgment and vindication, and so we should be ready.

The New Testament also refers to the new creation as "restoration" and "renewal." "He must remain in heaven until the time comes for God to *restore* everything, as he promised long ago through his holy prophets" (Acts 3:21, italics mine). "At the *renewal* of all things, when the Son of Man sits on his glorious throne, you who have followed me will also sit on twelve thrones" (Matt. 19:28, italics mine).

THE NEW HEAVEN AND EARTH

We are presented with one coherent picture: the end of all things is a restoration and renewal of heaven and earth. So forget the image of the soul of a human being lifting from a person's body at death to drift toward some ethereal, impersonal eternity. We can instead con-template Jesus' resurrection from the dead into a new and utterly transformed body. Heaven means real, ongoing personal existence, the ability to have genuine relationships, consciously communing with God in ways that we cannot even imagine because our worship is now limited by the earthiness of our life in this world.

Now, some people say that they see in the Bible a complete anni-hilation of the world, and images of nuclear holocaust make it easy to imagine. Didn't Jesus say, "Heaven and earth will pass away" (Matt. 24:35), and Isaiah, "All the stars of the heavens will be dis-solved and the sky rolled up like a scroll" (Isa. 34:4)? How about 2 Peter 3:12: "That day will bring about the destruction of the heav-ens by fire, and the elements will melt in the heat"? But this same passage goes on to say, "We are looking forward to a new heaven and a new earth, the home of righteousness" (v. 13).

Fire can mean judgment and purification, rather than annihila-tion of the universe. The dreadful promise and prediction of the day of the Lord goes back to the prophets and continues right through Jesus' teaching. It will be a time when evil is judged for what it is, and it will not be able to stand against the fire of God's judgment. Would any other outcome do? Do we not find ourselves looking for the final gavel in courtrooms, some decisive discernment of guilt and inno-cence, and do we not know that at the end of time as we know it, a divine gavel must fall? If there will be no moral clarity at the end of time, why should I look for any moral clarity now? We stand against a neighbor stealing our possessions or a teacher sexually abusing a student or a cop taking a bribe because justice is woven into the cre-ated world and will be fully revealed in the end.

Tragically, this means that those who have wanted nothing to do with God in this life, who have ignored him, insulted him, or inspired others to reject him, will get for eternity what they have chosen in this life. Hell is, in its essence, separation. Irreparable loss. It is us getting precisely what we wanted, if what we wanted in our lives was not to have the hassle of dealing with a Divine Sovereign, even though every requirement of that King is grace wrapped in love and mercy.

We cannot even imagine what the new heaven and earth will be like, but that existence is not about wading knee-deep in cloud and losing everything good we have ever known.

C. S. Lewis once said it bothered him that he didn't long for heaven more. We grow quite fond of things in this life, and often we get fonder the older we get. And then, he said, it struck him: maybe there is nothing he'd ever longed for that isn't heaven. What do we enjoy in this life? A vivacious creation, full of life and yet-to-be discovered mysteries. Friendships that are a true joy. Taste and touch, sight and sound and smell. Lewis was saying, "Isn't the view of the new heaven and earth as we get it from Scripture a promise of a fuller measure of just these things than we could ever experience in this life?" The life hereafter is life transformed and fulfilled, not life taken away. It is all of God's goodness emerging in a brand-new shape, but still having the same essential qualities of beauty, grace, and companionship.

In the Apocalypse of John, the exploding series of visions that reveal to us the meaning of things to come, we receive these symbols: no more sea (that is, no longer a world full of threats), God dwelling with man, no more tears, a new city, nations at peace, golden streets, a brilliant sun, and a new community merged with the heavenly beings. "The old order of things has passed away. . . . I am making everything new! . . . 'It is done'" (Rev. 21:4–6).

All this is the big "yet to come," and we live now in the "meantime." We can be encouraged by the empathy that comes through Romans 8 (yes, it is as if we are going through birth pains as we long for something better). We can get a head start on the new heaven and new earth: "If anyone is in Christ, he is a new creation; the old has gone, the new has come!" (2 Cor. 5:17).

Already come. That's something to hold on to.

PUTTING THE PIECES TOGETHER: WE'RE ALREADY THERE

It's a funny thing, but whenever I board an airplane to go to some faraway place, whenever I settle into that seat and buckle up, then feel myself pressed back into the seat as the plane shoots down the runway and then lifts its wheels off the bumpy concrete runway, I feel that I've already come to the place I'm going to. Maybe it's because air travel has so amazingly closed distances—almost like magic. Close your eyes, count to three, and you're there.

Maybe it's also like that in our conscious experience of the "here" and the "there," the "now and the "then," of hope.

If you have come to Christ as an ordinary person approaching him and choosing to believe in him, you have already come to the fulfillment of all he offers.

> But you have come to Mount Zion, to the heavenly Jerusalem, the city of the living God. You have come to thousands upon thousands of angels in joyful assembly, to the church of the firstborn, whose names are written in heaven. You have come to God, the judge of all men, to the spirits of righteous men made perfect, to Jesus the mediator of a new covenant, and to the sprinkled blood that speaks a better word than the blood of Abel.
>
> —Hebrews 12:22–24

The pieces have already come together.

PRAY THIS

Lord, I long for days when your goodness can be clearly seen above, and even within, the brokenness of this world. I groan because I long. I trust that you hold the future not just within your vision but also within your grasp. May I live now in such a way that I will know that I have already come to you, to a new community, and to the full forgiveness made possible by the blood of the Lord Jesus.

FOR REFLECTION OR DISCUSSION

1. What concept of heaven has been developing in your mind over the years, and how were that concept and those images formed?

2. If the new heaven and earth is the fulfillment of everything that is good in the first heaven and earth, what do you think it will bring to completion? In other words, what good things that God has done is he likely to keep doing in the future?

3. If the new creation includes the destruction of what is impure and against God's purposes, what would that include?

Patterns
Ways to Develop a God-Filled Life
Mel Lawrenz

*A good pattern progressively builds you up.
A bad pattern relentlessly erodes your
humanity.*

*Patterning is a focused commitment to
making a few habits and character traits the
normal, the daily, the consistent.*

All life is built in patterns. Nature has its
orderly patterns, from the bee building its
honeycomb to the DNA encoded in genes.
The Bible offers patterns for living a godly life. There are also patterns in every human life. As children of God, we have the power to choose the patterns we wish to follow. We can build patterns of behavior into our lives that shape our character, form our reputation, and determine our satisfaction in life.

You'll learn how to practice good life patterns that offer a design for spiritual health and strength, order for spiritual direction, and consistency for an intimate dialogue with God. Patterns challenges you to cultivate habits of life deeply rooted in the love and grace of God.

Patterns is a handbook for spiritual development that encourages you to discover the patterns of your own life—and how you can nurture God-inspired life patterns that build and strengthen your Christian faith.

Hardcover: 0-310-24810-8

Pick up a copy today at your favorite bookstore!

ZONDERVAN™

GRAND RAPIDS, MICHIGAN 49530 USA

WWW.ZONDERVAN.COM

We want to hear from you. Please send your comments about this book to us in care of zreview@zondervan.com. Thank you.

GRAND RAPIDS, MICHIGAN 49530 USA

WWW.ZONDERVAN.COM